# THE GROWTH ZONE

ALSO BY DAN STRUTZEL AND TRACI SHOBLOM

*The Power of Charisma*

*The Power of Positive Selling*

*Win!*

# THE GROWTH ZONE

## 30 DAYS TO RESET YOUR LIFE

DAN STRUTZEL &
TRACI SHOBLOM

Published 2026 by Gildan Media LLC
aka G&D Media
www.GandDmedia.com



Front cover design by David Rheinhardt of Pyrographx

Interior design by Meghan Day Healey of Story Horse, LLC.

Library of Congress Cataloging-in-Publication Data is available upon request

ISBN: 978-1-7225-0764-0

10 9 8 7 6 5 4 3 2 1

# CONTENTS

## Part Two

*The GROW! System for Change*



## Part Three

*The 30 Day GROW! Challenge*

# INTRODUCTION

## You Have the Power to Change Your Life

Two brothers, Stan and Barry, grew up in a regular middle class family. Like many brothers, they were polar opposites.

When Stan was a little boy, he would often tell his brother, "When I am bigger, I am going to be so happy. I'll be able to set my own bedtime, and eat whatever I want."

Then, as he grew, he'd say, "When I get into high school, I am going to be so happy. I'll have a car and can stay out later. I'll have a girlfriend. Yeah, I'll be happy in high school."

But, in high school, Stan said, "I am going to be so happy when I go off to college. My time will be my own. I can pick the classes I want, and stay out as late as I want."

By his senior year in college, Stan told his brother, "Oh man. I am going to be so happy to graduate. Carol and I are going to get married, and start a family, and I'll have a career. That's what I have been working for."

Unfortunately, the trend continued. For his whole life, Stan waited for some future point to be happy. "When the baby gets out of diapers . . ." "When I get that promotion at work." "When the kids are older and in school." "When I retire . . ."

On the last day of his life, Stan realized that he had waited too long to be happy. His life progressed, but he kept waiting for some point on the horizon when things would be perfect enough to be happy. He never felt empowered enough to make the changes he needed to be happy all along. And because of that, he didn't have a happy life.

Contrast that to Stan's brother Barry. From the get-go, his mother said he was a "happy baby." He was content playing with whatever toy he had in his hands . . . even if it was a wrapping paper tube. While his brother was waiting to be able to set his own bedtime, Barry sat under the covers with a flashlight, happy to have the quiet time to read. While Stan couldn't wait to get to high school so that he could have a car and a girlfriend, Barry enjoyed his neighbor friends and making cars out of things laying around the garage. In college, Barry got the most out of the experience, by playing in a band, studying hard for good grades, and exploring the campus. When it came time to graduate and get a job, Barry was excited to choose between two options. As soon as he walked in the front door of his new workplace, he found things to be happy about.

Growth opportunities were everywhere! Soon, Barry met a woman, got married, and had kids. He enjoyed every single moment of fatherhood.

When his own son started to grow up and become impatient for the future, Barry told him, "Son, a happy life is nothing more than a series of happy moments strung together. If you can't be happy now, you'll never be happy in the future. All we have is now."

*A happy life is just a series of happy moments strung together.*

Of course, this book is called *The Growth Zone* and not *The Happy Zone*. But, what is the purpose of growth, other than to obtain the knowledge, skills, attitudes, behaviors, and things that will make us happy? After all, no one is completely happy with their current state. There's always some area that could be improved. Maybe it's that twenty pounds you've been meaning to lose, or that beautiful home you want to buy. We all have growth goals. Some of us just have a higher "growth need" than others. Some of us don't care as much about changing and growing, and others are in constant search of something to learn, improve, or change.

Does that mean that a person with low growth needs is necessarily happier than a person with higher growth needs? Not at all. It's a matter of balancing out the desire for growth (whether it's a strong desire or a mild one) with the ability to be happy in the current state.

Part of that involves a person's belief in their ability to change. We'll call that "efficacy." A person with a high growth needs but a feeling that they don't have the power to change their circumstances is going to be less happy than a person with low growth needs who believes that he or she can change things if they want to. Similarly, a person with high growth needs and the confidence that they can achieve their goals is likely to be happy. And the person with low growth needs but doesn't feel that they can change things anyway is likely to be neutral.

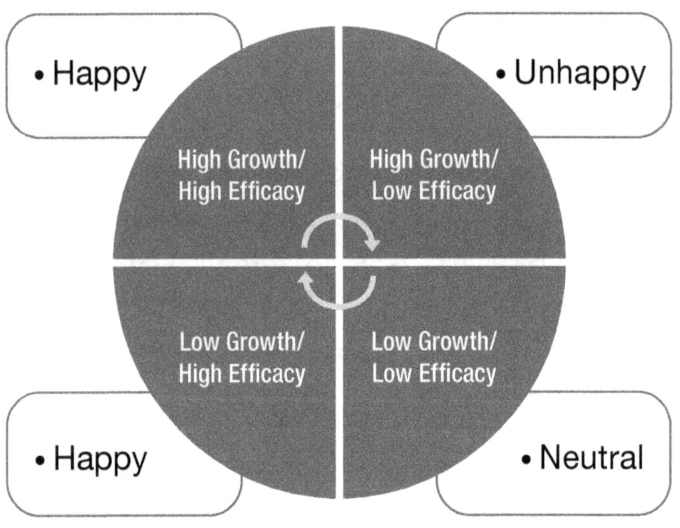


So, how do we balance out having goals for the future with being happy in the moment? That's what this book is about. *The Growth Zone: 30 Days to Reset Your Life* isn't only about changing the things that need changing in your life. It's also about being happy every day, while you're growing. And, sometimes the growth comes in changing the way you see your current situation. After all, there are some things we can change in life, and some things we can't. It's the old Serenity Prayer, written by Reinhold Niebuhr in the mid 1900s:

*God grant me the serenity to accept the things I cannot change;*
*the courage to change the things I can;*
*and the wisdom to know the difference.*

---

*If you can't change something about your life, you can change the way you feel about it.*

---

Here's how a Growth Mindset, which is the vehicle that allows you to enter The Growth Zone, will help you do just that. (For the sake of simplicity, we'll refer to a Growth Mindset as "GROW!") First, we'll tap into the power of your mind and make sure that the timing is right for growth. Then, in Part One, we'll lay the foundation for growth by looking at your comfort zone and how it might be keeping you stuck. We'll explore the growth cycle, and identify the four keys to lasting change. To use a garden metaphor, it's about preparing the soil and choosing the right time to plant.

In Part Two, we'll get into the GROW! System for Change. GROW is an acronym for Goals, Realign, Overcome obstacles, and Work. These chapters will, using our gardening metaphor, plant the seeds of growth, and then nurture the seedling until it grows into a strong, deeply rooted plant.

Finally, in Part Three, we'll put the system to work, with a 30 Day GROW! Challenge. Here you'll have an opportunity to implement everything you've learned so that your life is appreciably different in just one month.

Are you ready to get started? Let's GROW!

# CHAPTER ONE
# Tap into Your Power

*"I could not, at any age, be content to take my place by the fireside and simply look on. Life was meant to be lived. Curiosity must be kept alive. One must never, for whatever reason, turn his back on life."*

—Eleanor Roosevelt

Did you know that you have the ability to tap into the same force that made Martin Luther King Jr., Mahatma Gandhi, and Winston Churchill incredible leaders? It's the same power that allowed Walt Disney to overcome numerous rejections and build the Disney empire. It's the power to change your life from where it is now to the life you want to be living.

How can you tap into this great power? You already have. It comes in those moments when everything is flowing; when you know nothing could go wrong. It's those days when you feel attractive and confident, others notice you, you get the best parking space, the elevator is already there . . .

You've also experienced the opposite. You've had times when nothing seemed sure. Everything seemed out of your control. You went from a bad morning to a worse day.

What's the difference between tapping into your power and feeling powerless? The difference is focus. What we choose to focus our attention on is what will grow. When we spend our precious mental energy thinking negative thoughts ("I am so tired today. My back hurts. The car is dirty again. How come no one ever helps me around here?") we tend to notice more things to be negative about.

Similarly, when we focus on good things ("Wow look at that sunrise. I really like his tie. I think that project turned out really well. I'm excited to have spaghetti for dinner.") those are the things we tend to notice more of.

It may sound a bit shocking, but the outside world is not the source of your power. Sure, external circumstances do happen that affect you. We're not suggesting that you go live on a mountaintop and withdraw from life. But, really, the source of your power lies within you. It lives in your ability to change how you feel by changing the way you look at your current circumstances. Another way of putting it is to say that, "The seeds of your future life are in your life today." And your positive attention is the water that grows the seeds of your life.

*The seeds of your future life are in your life today.*

## Locus of Control

In psychology, there is a concept called Locus of Control. It's a mindset that reflects how much control a person feels about his or her ability to effect a specific outcome. Locus of control is a term used to define whether or not a person perceives they have control over the events in their lives. An *external locus of control* means that a person feels that he or she doesn't control the events in life but that the control lies outside of him or her. A person with this belief thinks that he or she is either "lucky" or "unlucky" and that things just happen to him or her.

An *internal locus of control* means that a person feels in control or that he or she can directly influence the events that happen. People with this belief system think that they are ultimately in control of their own destiny and that the actions they take can influence the events of their lives.

But, what's interesting is that people with external locus of control tend to focus on different things than people with internal locus of control. In our Stan and Barry example from the Introduction, both boys were raised in the exact same environment, but each child focused on different things. Stan was focused on what he didn't have in his current life (a car, freedom), whereas Barry was focused on the positive he did have. Stan had external locus of control because he was always waiting for the next thing that was going to make him happy. Barry had internal locus of control because he knew he could be happy no matter what the circumstance.

So, how can you learn to be more of a Barry and less of a Stan? By consciously choosing what filter you use to perceive information.

## Filters

In the book *Listen: The Art of Effective Communication,* by Dale Carnegie & Associates, the author discusses the idea of filters. "A filter is a conscious choice to focus more on one thing than another. Using our photography example, the filter is what the camera lens chooses to focus on—what areas are sharp and what are blurry, what areas are light and which are darkened?"

In the book, there is a great example of how filters can affect perception. Two people walk into a room where there is a huge glass window that looks out to a 180-degree panoramic ocean view.

Mary says, "Look at that view of the ocean!"

Bill says, "I can barely see out the window, with all the dirt on it. Someone should really clean it."

Mary replies, "Can you imagine seeing the sun streaming in like that every morning when you wake up?"

Bill answers, "I can imagine that it would be too bright in the morning. And, where is the privacy? I would definitely need curtains."

Mary in this instance is focusing on what is outside the window—the ocean, the sunlight streaming in. Bill is focusing on the window itself. Mary has a positive view of the large window that looks outside because she is filtering out the dirty window and the lack of privacy. Bill has a negative view of the large window that looks outside because he is filtering out the beautiful view. Instead, he is focusing on the need for curtains, the need for clean windows, and the lack of privacy.

Which of these two people is more likely to feel inspired, positive, and powerful? Mary, because she is focusing on what is positive. Bill is less likely to be happy because he is filtering out the good things and focusing on what needs changing.

Does this mean that Bill is wrong? Should he just overlook the dirty window, the bright sun, and the lack of privacy? Of course not. Choosing to focus on the positive doesn't mean having a Pollyanna view of life. Windows need cleaning. Curtains need hanging. But if your natural tendency is to focus on what's missing, what's lacking, and what's wrong, you are more likely to feel powerless. And that attention to what's missing will only serve to grow your focus on other things that are missing in your life.

## The Mirror Rule

Have you ever noticed what happens when you go see a really great movie? One that is inspiring, or funny, or romantic? You leave the theater in a great mood. Everything seems better, brighter, and annoyances such as traffic or delays don't bother you as much.

Conversely, if you've just seen an emotionally dramatic movie, it affects your mood as well. Everything seems to take on nuanced meaning as you see the world through the lens of the movie you just saw. "People are selfish and cruel." "Don't trust anyone . . ."

Why is that? The reason that movies affect our mindset so strongly has to do with something called The Mirror Rule.

In his book, *Flicker: Your Brain on Movies,* Jeffrey Zacks, a professor of psychology and director of the Dynamic Cognition Laboratory at Washington University in St. Louis says the following about the impact movies have on our minds*:

"One way that we perceive emotion in film is through a process I call the Mirror Rule, which says that it's a good idea to mimic the visual input that you're seeing. So if you walk up to somebody and they smile at you, it's good to smile back.

"If you watch somebody in the theater and there's a smiling face filling the screen, most of the audience is going to pop a little bit of a smile.

* https://www.today.com/health/your-brain-movies-why-films-make-us-cry-flinch-cheer-1D80258284

"When we're smiling, we tend to feel happier. When we're frowning, we tend to feel angrier. So that combination of the Mirror Rule and the reading of emotion by the brain off the current state of the body is enough to produce emotion."

So, what happens, then, is we leave the theater, and our minds have been mirroring certain emotions for two or more hours, and we continue to process information through that filter. You see a movie with a positive filter, your mind will continue to filter out the bad and filter in the good. You see a depressing movie and you're more likely to filter out good things and attend to depressing or sad things.

## Changing the Filter

How can you learn to change the filter through which you are seeing things? By consciously looking for the seeds of your future life that are present in your current life.

Are you looking for a great relationship? Start behaving as if you were in a fantastic loving relationship. Set aside a weekly date night, and take YOURSELF out to dinner and a movie. Focus on the great relationships and love you already have.

Do you want a coaching practice full of clients? Set aside office hours and sit at your desk and focus on how you already create value and coach people, even if it's not for money.

Maybe you want wealth and abundance? Start focusing your positive attention on the wealth and abundance that already exists in your life. Don't think that you already have wealth and abundance? Take a look at third world countries. You see people who are strapping on pieces of cardboard for shoes and suddenly you'll feel like Bill Gates.

So here's how to do it.

Decide what you want your future life to look like. We'll get more into the specifics on that in Part Two of this book. Once you've decided on an area where you want to grow, then take a look in your present life for the seeds of that.

Be thrilled, happy, and grateful for those tiny seeds. Not for what they are GOING to become but for what they already are.

Also, manage your mood. When you notice that you're focusing on the negative in a situation, and it's leading you down a path of negativity, break the pattern. Stop what you're doing, go get a drink of water if you can, and literally tell yourself, "I'm focusing on the negative. What's good in this situation?" If you can't find anything good in the situation at hand, then find something else to feel good about. Soon, your mind will start to mirror the good mood, and you'll be back in a positive mind set.

Here's an example. You're at work in a meeting when one of your colleagues presents an idea that you told her about the week before. She's presenting it as if it were her idea. One of the areas you've identified you want to work on is being more assertive at work, but when she starts taking credit for your idea, your heart sinks. You start to think, "Of course she stole my idea. People are always stealing my ideas. Although most of my ideas aren't worth stealing anyway. I should just let her have the idea. I probably wouldn't have explained it right anyway."

Your mood continues to drop as the meeting progresses. Your mind wanders. "Remember your last performance evaluation? It was really mediocre. There's no way I am ever going to get promoted with scores like that."

What can you do to turn it around? Your mood is sinking fast and you're starting to feel powerless to change your life.

"Pardon me, I'm going to step out to use the restroom." Then, in your mind, change your frame. "Look. We said we wanted to be more assertive. Remember last week when the neighbor parked in our space and we said something about it, and they apologized? That's a seed right there. Let's go in there and do it again."

You walk back in the meeting, and they are still talking about the idea. When there is a lull in the conversation, you say something like, "I just want to say how glad I am that the conversation is going in this direction. In fact, when I mentioned this idea to Darla last week, she thought it was a great idea then. Thanks, Darla, for bringing it up today."

Suddenly, you feel proud. You're happy you stood up for yourself and are growing a skill that you want to grow. The rest of the day is likely to be much better than it would have been if you hadn't consciously shifted your filter from powerless to empowered.

Tapping into your power and shifting your focus simply requires a conscious effort to notice the seeds of your future life that are present in your current life, and put your attention on them.

In the next chapter, we'll delve into your readiness and the timing of growth.

# CHAPTER TWO
# Are You Ready to Grow?

*"I learned that we can do anything, but we can't do everything . . . at least not at the same time. So think of your priorities not in terms of what activities you do, but when you do them. Timing is everything."*

—Author Dan Millman

Imagine it's the Monday before Thanksgiving (pre-Covid, of course). You have a big family dinner coming up and you go to buy some new pants so that Aunt Edna doesn't give you a hard time about what you're wearing again this year. You're in the dressing room trying things on when you come to a horrible realization. You've gained weight and have gone up an entire size. I *need to go on a diet*, you think. Do you start a new diet three days before Thanksgiving?

Or, it's Friday afternoon, before a holiday weekend, and everyone is rushing to get their work done so they can leave the office. You have been meaning to ask your boss to give you a raise, and have even prepared some documents to demonstrate your value to the company. You figure it'll take about twenty minutes to go through them and ask for the raise. Do you go in there now and do it?

Finally, you've always wanted to go to graduate school and get your MBA. Your spouse has always been really encouraging with your life and career goals, but the program would require a lot of time and energy—not to mention money. Plus, you have been thinking about starting a family and worry about juggling the demands of school and parenthood. Should you apply to the program now?

The answers to these questions depend on two things. Are you internally ready to make the change, and is the external environment one that is supportive of the change?

## Timing is Everything

As we have all experienced, there are some times in life that are better than others to initiate change. It's probably not a good idea to go on a diet three days before an eating holiday, or to ask your boss for a raise if she is distracted.

Whether you can handle an MBA and a young child, though, isn't as clear cut. That's a matter of your own personal characteristics and the environment. Are you resourceful? Adaptable? Adventurous? These are some traits that can mitigate the effect of the environment.

## Lewin's Equation

In 1936, social Psychologist Kurt Lewin created a simple equation that tells us a lot about why we do what we do.

$$B = f(p,e)$$

*Behavior is a function of the person and the environment.*

This idea, now known as Lewin's Equation, gives us a deep understanding about the factors that influence our behavior. Before Lewin came up with this, people thought that a person's actions were a result of the kind of person they are. If a person is on a diet but goes off of it a few days into it, we might think, "They don't have any willpower."

But, Lewin's Equation says that there is more to the story. Our behavior is a function of our own personal characteristics *and* the environment. In other words, maybe the person went off the diet because it was the holidays and there were a lot of environmental triggers.

In order to effectively change, we need to address both the INTERNAL and EXTERNAL factors that affect the change. You can be the most motivated person in the world, but if the environmental factors are not supportive (such as timing), the change is unlikely to stick. Similarly, it can be the perfect time to grow, but if you don't have the right mindset, you're not likely to succeed.

## Fixed Mindset versus Growth Mindset

Carol Dweck, a Stanford professor, describes the differences between a fixed mindset and a growth mindset. When you are using a fixed mindset, you believe that your abilities in a particular area are fixed. When you are using a growth mindset, you believe that you can improve, learn, and build upon your current abilities.

*In a fixed mindset students believe their basic abilities, their intelligence, their talents, are just fixed traits. They have a certain amount and that's that, and then their goal becomes to look smart all the time and never look dumb. In a growth mindset students understand that their talents and abilities can be developed through effort, good teaching and persistence. They don't necessarily think everyone's the same or anyone can be Einstein, but they believe everyone can get smarter if they work at it.*

—Carol Dweck, Stanford University*

One interesting thing is that growth mindset and fixed mindset aren't static. In other words, a person doesn't necessarily ALWAYS have a growth mindset or a fixed mindset. There are certain areas of life where we may feel that our areas are fixed and other areas where we believe we can grow and change.

In other words, Laura may think of herself as "bad at writing." She has a fixed mindset about it, and doesn't believe that she'll ever be a "good writer" no matter

* www.onedublin.org/2012/06/19/stanford-universitys-carol-dweck-on-the-growth-mindset-and-education/

how hard she tries. On the other hand, Laura is learning how to play the piano, and believes that with good instruction and lots of practice, she can make beautiful music. She has a growth mindset about musical ability.

Professor T.J. Jenney identified seven traits of change readiness. These are by no means the only traits that determine whether or not you are ready to grow, but they do cover the core internal factors.

## Seven Traits of Change Readiness*

**1. Resourcefulness:** Resourceful people are effective at taking the most of any situation and utilizing whatever resources are available to develop plans and contingencies. They see more than one way to achieve a goal, and they're able to look in less obvious places to find help. They have a real talent for creating new ways to solve old problems.

When people low in resourcefulness encounter obstacles, they get stuck, dig in their heels, and go back to the old way. People high in resourcefulness might overlook obvious solutions and create more work than is necessary.

**2. Optimism:** Is the glass half empty or half full? Optimism is highly correlated with Change-Readiness, since the pessimist observes only problems and obstacles while the optimist recognizes opportunities and possibilities.

---

* From a website for a leadership class taught by Associate Professor T. J. Jenney at Purdue www.tech.purdue.edu/ols/courses/ols386/crispo/changereadinesstest.doc

Optimists tend to be more enthusiastic and positive about change. Their positive outlook is, founded on an abiding faith in the future and the belief that things usually work out for the best. Very high optimism scorers may lack critical-thinking skills.

**3. Adventurousness:** Two ingredients capture this adventurous spirit: the *inclination to take risks and* the *desire to pursue the unknown*, to walk the path less taken. Adventurous people love a challenge.

Since change always involves both risk and the unknown, they usually perform well during organizational shake-ups. They are the proactors, the employees who initiate and create change. But very high scores on adventurousness may indicate a tendency toward recklessness.

**4. Passion/Drive:** Passion is the fuel that maximizes all the other traits. If you have passion, nothing appears impossible. If you don't, change is exhausting. Passion is the individual's level of personal dynamism. It shows up in a person's level of intensity and determination.

To make a new procedure work, to overcome the myriad of problems that any plan for change unwittingly produces, you've got to have passion and enthusiasm. Very high scores on passion/drive, however, may mean you're bullheaded, obsessed, and heading for burnout.

**5. Adaptability:** Adaptability includes two elements: flexibility and resilience. Flexible people have goals and dreams like everyone else, but they're not overly invested in them. When something doesn't work out, they'll say, "Plan A doesn't work, let's go to Plan B." Resilience is the capacity to rebound from adversity quickly with a minimum of trauma. Failure or mistakes do not throw them. They don't dwell on them and get depressed but bounce back quickly and move on.

High scorers on this trait are not wedded to specific outcomes. If the situation changes, their expectations shift right along with it. Scoring too high in this trait indicates a lack of commitment or stick-to-it-ness.

**6. Confidence:** If optimism is the view that a situation will work out, confidence is the belief in your own ability to handle it. There is situational confidence—"I know I can swim across this channel, learn this program, write this report"—and self-confidence—"I can handle whatever comes down the pike." Self-confidence is the kind of confidence the Change Readiness Scale measures.

High scorers are generally individuals with a strong sense of self-esteem. But more specifically, they believe they can make any situation work for them. Scorers above 26 may indicate a cocky, know-it-all attitude and lack of receptivity to feedback.

**7. Tolerance for Ambiguity:** The one certainty surrounding change is that it spawns uncertainty. No matter how carefully you plan it, there is always an element of indefiniteness or ambiguity.

Without a healthy tolerance for ambiguity, change is not only uncomfortable; it's downright scary. But too much tolerance can also get you in trouble. You may have difficulty finishing tasks and making decisions.

Now it's your turn. On the next page is the Change Readiness Assessment. This measures the internal readiness to change, not the external environment.

We learned that behavior is a function of the person and the environment. Short of being aware of the environmental factors and timing the change appropriately, we really aren't in control of our environmental factors. But, we can work on the internal traits that can lead to success, and that can tip the scales.

## Change-Readiness Assessment

On a scale from 1–6, rate how accurately the statement describes you; where 1 is not like you at all, and 6 is exactly like you.

___ 1. I prefer the familiar to the unknown.
___ 2. I rarely second-guess myself.
___ 3. I'm unlikely to change plans once they're set.
___ 4. I can't wait for the day to get started.
___ 5. I believe in not getting your hopes too high.
___ 6. If something's broken, I try to find a way to fix it.
___ 7. I get impatient when there are no clear answers.
___ 8. I'm inclined to establish routines and stay with them.
___ 9. I can make any situation work for me.
___ 10. When something important doesn't work out, it takes me time to adjust.
___ 11. I have a hard time relaxing and doing nothing.
___ 12. If something can go wrong, it usually does.
___ 13. When I get stuck I'm inclined to improvise solutions.
___ 14. I get frustrated when I can't get a grip on something.
___ 15. I prefer work that is similar and in my comfort zone.
___ 16. I can handle anything that comes along.
___ 17. Once I've made up my mind, I don't easily change it.

___ 18. I push myself to the max.
___ 19. My tendency is to focus on what can go wrong.
___ 20. When people need solutions to problems, they call on me.
___ 21. When an issue is unclear, my impulse is to clarify it right away.
___ 22. It pays to stay with the tried and true.
___ 23. I focus on my strengths not my weaknesses.
___ 24. I find it hard to give up on something even if it's not working out.
___ 25. I'm restless and full of energy.
___ 26. Things rarely work out the way you want them to.
___ 27. My strength is to find ways around obstacles.
___ 28. I can't stand to leave things unfinished.
___ 29. I prefer the main highway to the backroad.
___ 30. My faith in my abilities is unshakable.
___ 31. When in Rome, do as the Romans do.
___ 32. I'm a vigorous and passionate person.
___ 33. I'm more likely to see problems than opportunities.
___ 34. I look in unusual places to find solutions.
___ 35. I don't perform well when there are vague expectations and goals.

## Scoring

Add the scores for the questions in each category as indicated below. Note: Optimal range for all categories is between 22 and 26.

**RESOURCEFULNESS**

6. ______
13. ______
20. ______
27. ______
34. ______

Total ______

**CONFIDENCE**

2. ______
9. ______
16. ______
23. ______
30. ______

Total ______

**PASSION/DRIVE**

4. ______
11. ______
18. ______
25. ______
32. ______

Total ______

**ADAPTABILITY**

3. ______
10. ______
17. ______
24. ______
31. ______

Total ______

**ADVENTUROUSNESS**

1. ______
8. ______
15. ______
22. ______
29. ______

Total ______

**OPTIMISM**

5. ______
12. ______
19. ______
26. ______
33. ______

Total ______

**TOLERANCE FOR AMBIGUITY**

7. ______
14. ______
21. ______
28. ______
35. ______

Total ______

## Your Profile:

Write down your scores for each category.

Resourcefulness ________

Adaptability ________

Optimism ________

Confidence ________

Adventurousness ________

Tolerance for Ambiguity ________

Passion/Drive ________

You'll probably find you have higher scores on some traits and lower scores on others. This is typical of most profiles and indicates that some of your Change-Readiness traits are more developed than others.

Look at the areas that are lower than the ideal. These are the areas to strengthen as you're getting ready to grow.

As Dale Carnegie said, "First ask yourself, what is the worst that can happen? Then, prepare to accept it and proceed to improve upon the worst."

In the next chapter, we'll talk about something familiar to all of us—the comfort zone.

---

*"First ask yourself, what is the worst that can happen? Then, prepare to accept it and proceed to improve upon the worst."*

---

# Part One

## *Laying the Foundation for Growth*

# CHAPTER THREE
# The Comfort Zone

*"Most everything that you want is just outside your comfort zone. Everything you want is out there waiting for you to ask. Everything you want also wants you. But you have to take action to get it." "Our job is not to figure out the 'how'. The 'how' will show up out of the commitment and belief in the 'what.'"*

—Jack Canfield

Peter and Robert are two college professors at the same university. They both have tenure, which means that they have a high level of job security. It's very hard to fire a professor who has tenure.

Both men are good at their jobs and like them. Sure, it gets a bit mundane teaching the same subjects again and again every year. But the work is comfortable, safe and secure.

Along comes an opportunity for them both to leave their roles as tenured professors to teach at a startup university. The pay would be not quite as good, and there wouldn't be any tenure, but it would be a chance to grow a new school from the ground up.

Peter and Robert are both in what's called "the comfort zone." It's a psychological state where things feel familiar to a person and they are at ease and in control of their environment, and experience low levels of stress and anxiety.

The idea of a comfort zone has scientific backing from the Yerkes-Dodson Law,* discovered by two researchers in 1908. They found that there is a relationship between arousal and performance. Performance increases with physiological or mental arousal, but only up to a point. After that, you get overly stressed out, and performance starts to decline. It resembles an upside down U. Just the right amount of arousal, and we get energized and excited. Novelty is associated with increased performance. But, then there is a tipping point. Performance goes down because we get cognitively stressed out. Our bodies release stress hormones, and we aren't as able to think, react, or solve problems.

## Levels of Arousal and Individual Differences

The shape of the inverted U curve varies depending on a few factors. Different tasks require different levels of arousal. For example, difficult or intellectually demanding tasks may require a lower level of arousal (to facilitate concentration), whereas tasks demanding

* https://en.wikipedia.org/wiki/Yerkes%E2%80%93Dodson_law

stamina or persistence may be performed better with higher levels of arousal (to increase motivation).

So, when you're writing a book, for example, you need lower levels of arousal so you can concentrate (but still have a deadline to meet so there is SOME arousal) than if you are running a marathon (where you need motivation to make it through).

There are also individual differences in the amount of arousal a person needs/wants, and at what point is the top of that inverted U.

So, in our example above, Peter prefers to stay inside his comfort zone because the risk of losing his tenure, some of his income, and the security of a job he knows how to do well provides too much arousal. Unlike Robert, Peter has two kids in college. "Maybe someday I'll be in a position to take a job like that. But right now, the risk is too high."

Robert, on the other hand, has a different shaped curve. He is energized by the possibility, and doesn't see tenure or job security as important as Peter does. This allows him to step outside of his comfort zone, give up his tenured position, and "go for" something new.

## Who Was Right?

This begs the question, who made the better decision? Peter or Robert? Neither of them! A comfort zone isn't good or bad, it's just a psychological state. As we mentioned in the last chapter, sometimes the timing isn't right to pursue a particular growth opportunity.

There is nothing wrong with changing a goal, or delaying one until a better time. It doesn't mean you'll never achieve the goal, but frankly, if it's almost April, and you haven't made progress on a goal you started in January, then there is probably some reason why that is the case.

## The Difference Between Reasons and Excuses

There is a big difference between reasons and excuses. A reason is a legitimate answer as to why you haven't been able to achieve a goal. "I didn't train for the marathon because I broke my leg." That is a reason. "I didn't train for the marathon because I didn't have time" is probably an excuse.

So, are there legitimate reasons why you haven't achieved your goal, or are you making excuses?

In other words, when you think of your goal, you need to listen to what you are telling yourself. That voice is going to tell you the true reality of why you aren't moving forward with that goal. You'll be able to hear whether you have reasons, or are making excuses.

## How do you recognize an excuse?

It usually goes like "I can't _______ because _______."

Another variation is, "That won't work because _______."

Usually we use the word "because" in our excuses. Whenever you hear yourself say the word "because" pay attention. Did you just make an excuse?

## How to turn excuses into "Whys"

Find an inspiration of someone who did or does what you are saying you can't do. It doesn't have to be a someone famous. How about that lady down at the church who manages to run the youth program even though she works two jobs? Or your sister in law who lost 75 pounds when she found out she was diabetic. Find someone who inspires you.

---

*When you hear yourself making excuses, think of that person.*

---

If there are legitimate reasons why you haven't made progress on your goal, then maybe this isn't the right time to focus on achieving it. Achieving a goal takes a lot of time, energy and focus. That's not an excuse, it's a reality. If you're not in a place right now where you can devote the energy necessary to achieving your goal, then don't. Get through whatever is going on, and then start on the goal.

So for example, if you are a graduate student, and a mother to four kids, and also have a full time job, now is probably not the right time to start in on that weight loss, stop smoking, exercise program. It's the truth. Don't beat yourself up about it. Just accept the fact that you have other goals that are more important right now—like getting through school.

However, if the time never seems right, there is always something that comes up, and your goal never seems to make it to the top of your priority list, then you are making excuses. It's time to take a deeper look. There is a reason you are avoiding this goal, and in order to move forward, you're going to need to find out what that reason is. Maybe you're scared. Maybe you don't feel like you deserve to achieve the goal. Maybe there are other implications of reaching that goal that you aren't ready to deal with yet.

## Accepting What Is

You can change your life, but in order to do that, you've got to accept what is. If "what is" is that you're afraid, you don't think you can do it, you're not even really sure you want that goal, then that's where you need to start. Back off on yourself for awhile, and take a look at those thoughts. Don't try to positive-think your way out of them. You need to look at those limiting beliefs and examine them.

You are not achieving your goal. That is. *Why* are you not achieving your goal? That's where you start to ask the questions. Maybe you need to put that goal on hold for awhile while you are laying a new foundation of beliefs to support it. You see, just as you can't build a house on a faulty foundation, you can't achieve a goal if you don't have the inner foundation to support it.

---

*If you are consistently not achieving your goal, it's probably because you haven't built an inner foundation that will support the long term achievement of that goal.*

---

Before you can climb on that treadmill, you need to go inside your head and find out what the thoughts are that are supporting your thunder thighs, and then change those into thoughts that support a healthy lifestyle. **You have to change your thinking before you can change your life.**

It's like those stories about lottery winners who blow all of their money. Why? Why does that happen? It's everyone's fantasy to win a huge sum of money. And every single one of us says "Oh I wouldn't be one of those who blows all the money." But, if the winners don't have a solid belief system that includes an inner image of themselves as a wealthy person, the money is going to go. You've got to have an inner mindset that is consistent with your outer goal.

So, how do you do that? How do you create an inner foundation to support that external goal? You get out of the comfort zone, and into "the zone."

## Out of the Comfort Zone and into the Zone

What is "The Zone?" It's when your subconscious takes over your performance and you aren't aware of what you're doing.

Walking
Riding a bike
Playing the piano
Skating
Typing

The Zone is as automatic as the comfort zone, but is characterized by enhanced performance.

There are three aspects of The Zone:

**Physical**—This is when you are performing at a high level of excellence effortlessly.

**Mental**—This is when brilliant ideas come to you—insights, thoughts, "a ha" moments.

**Spiritual**—This comes as a feeling of one-ness with whatever you call God.

TO GET INTO THE ZONE:

1. Have clear goals for what you want to accomplish
2. Practice!! Make the behaviors automatic.
3. Create an environment where you can concentrate completely and have the appropriate amount of arousal for the task, and your personality.
4. Breathe, relax, and LET GO. Getting in the zone is more about "letting go" than anything.

YOU'LL KNOW YOU'RE THERE WHEN:

1. You experience a distorted sense of time—"has it really already been 2 hours!"
2. You lose your sense of complete personal control over the activity "It just flowed through me."
3. You have a loss of the feeling of self-consciousness, the merging of action and awareness.

Pretty soon, you are going to find yourself effortlessly taking steps toward your goals. It won't be a matter of making yourself do stuff. It will be a matter of living out the inner belief system you have. Change does not happen from the outside in. It happens from the inside out.

---

*A goal is not something you should do. It's an opportunity to move your life forward.*

---

# CHAPTER FOUR
## The Growth Cycle

*We grew up on the same street,*
*You and me.*
*We went to the same schools,*
*Rode the same bus,*
*Had the same friends,*
*And even shared spaghetti*
*With each other's families.*
*And though our roots belong to*
*The same tree,*
*Our branches have grown*
*In different directions.*
*Our tree,*
*Now resembles a thousand*
*Other trees*
*In a sea of a trillion*
*Other trees*
*With parallel destinies*
*And similar dreams.*
*You cannot envy the branch*

*That grows bigger*
*From the same seed,*
*And you cannot*
*Blame it on the sun's direction.*
*But you still compare us,*
*As if we're still those twos*
*Kids at the park*
*Slurping down slushies and*
*Eating ice cream.*
—SUZY KASSEM, *Rise Up and Salute the Sun*

This incredible poem captures the essence of personal and professional growth. Every one of us has had several "lifetimes" within one life. Then, the structure of that life changes, for one reason or another, and we build another life from the seeds of that one. The seed grows into a tree. The tree develops branches. The branches drop their own seeds, and new trees form from that.

## The Structure of Revolution

In Thomas Kuhn's classic book, *The Structure of Scientific Revolutions*, he talks about the process of change.* Although he writes within the context of science, the ideas also apply to personal and professional growth. In his model, there is an existing paradigm—the status quo. But, over time, anomalies to current thinking

* https://www.uky.edu/~eushe2/Pajares/Kuhn.html

appear. We learn new things that make us realize that the old way of doing things or understanding is outdated. Pretty soon, there are so many anomalies that the old paradigm can't exist anymore. It falls apart into chaos. This is why change is so scary, for most people. There's usually an intense period of chaos after initiating a change, which causes some people to retreat back into the comfort zone.

But, chaos can't last. Nature prefers order. So, from the chaos comes a new paradigm that fits the new insights and understanding. The cycle begins again.

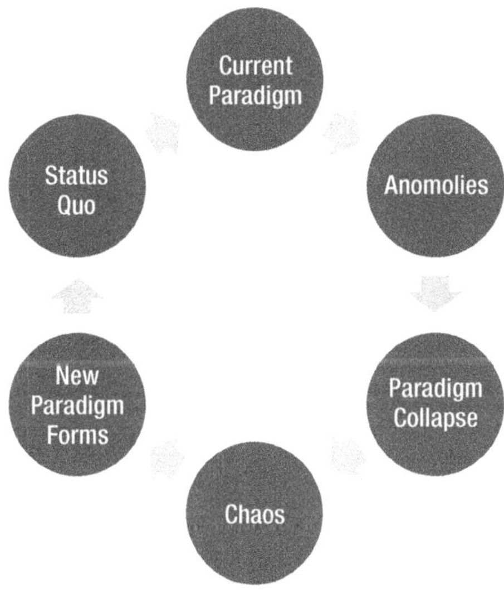


## Four Key Stages

Through coaching thousands of people over the years, we have identified that there are four key stages of personal growth, to address when a person wants to make a change that is lasting.

First, the person needs to be ***sufficiently unhappy with their current state***. In order to make lasting change, you've got to feel the pain of your current situation—but not too much. As we learned in the previous chapter, if you don't feel any pain at all, you aren't motivated to change. If you feel too much, you get overwhelmed and shut down and retreat back into your comfort zone.

## How *Not* to "Feel the Pain"

Let's say you did let yourself feel the pain. You got a realistic glimpse of how serious the problem is. Now what?

Many people fall immediately into a negative pattern of thinking. "I am a horrible person." "There is no way I am ever going to change this, why even try?"

This is the wrong thing to do! The second key to making lasting change is that a person ***needs to believe that they are capable of making the change***. If you find that you are beating yourself up, then you are not ready to change yet. While it's important to get a realistic picture of your problem, if you are going to use that information to make yourself feel worse, then you're not going to be able to make changes.

One way to tell whether or not you're ready to change is to listen to your internal communication after you "feel the pain." A person who is ready for change will say to themselves, "Wow. This is bad. I can't believe I let it get to this point. I have got to do something about this *now*, because I cannot stand living this way one more day." That is the attitude of someone who is ready to commit to lasting change.

If you're not there yet, that's okay. Just focus on changing your filter and getting into the right mindset.

This leads us to the third key in making lasting change. ***You need to know what to do to achieve the goal.*** Now, with some goals, it's obvious. To lose weight, for example, you need to move more and eat less. Of course, just because it's obvious doesn't mean it's easy!

With some goals, though, what you need to do to achieve that goal is less obvious.

For example, many people have a goal to "become a millionaire." In one sense, that's a good goal because it's concrete. You can easily tell when you have a million dollars because you can look at your financial statements and see the evidence of it. However, most people don't have a clue what they need to do to achieve that goal. How do you make a million dollars? There are hundreds of ways, of course. But how *you* are going to do it might be unclear.

This leads us to the fourth, and final key to making lasting changes. **You need to build your goal into your daily life.** How can you do that? Let's look at another idea from the brilliant researcher Kurt Lewin.

## Resisting Forces and Driving Forces

Kurt Lewin (the same guy from The Lewin Equation) developed a concept in change management known as

Force Field Analysis. In the model, two types of forces are examined: those that promote change and those that resist change. The forces that promote change are called *driving forces*, and those that attempt to maintain the status quo are called *restraining forces* or *resisting forces.* According to the model, in order for any change to occur, the driving forces must exceed the restraining forces, thus upsetting the equilibrium.

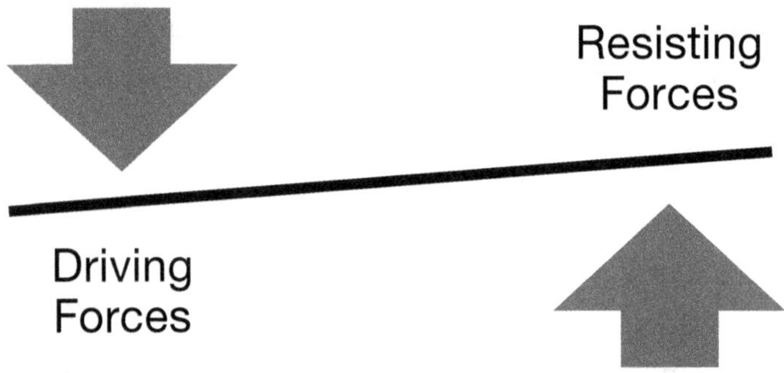


Some examples of driving forces in, say, health care, are things like technological advancement, cutting-edge research, the development of new medications, and other things that promote change and progress.

Some examples of restraining forces in health care would include governmental regulation, lack of money and financing, political and social resistance, and other things that slow down progress.

If you want to make a lasting change in health-care, then the driving forces must be stronger than the resisting forces.

## Lewin's Change Model

So, how can you use this idea to strengthen the driving forces for change in your everyday life?

Lewin's Change Model has three steps:

1. **Unfreezing:** This is reducing the strength of the resisting forces.
2. **Moving:** This is increasing the strength of the driving forces.
3. **Refreezing:** This is stabilizing after the change has been made so that there is a new equilibrium.

In order to effect lasting change, all three of these need to be considered. Specifically, something needs to be done to reduce the strength of the resisting force, increase the strength of the driving forces, and then help freeze the equilibrium again after the change.

Let's look at an example.

Stuart is a front line manager for a national bookstore. With the advent of internet publishing, e-book, and online retailers, business is down, and his hours are being cut back. What used to be a job that kept his family fed and comfortable now barely pays the bills.

His wife Katie calls him at work one day and says, "Stu, the car just died and the mechanic says that it will cost more to fix it than to replace it. What are we going to do? I need a car to take the kids to their schools!"

*That's it,* Stuart thinks. I *have had enough. I need to do something to fix my financial situation. We can't go on living like this.*

Stuart is now in the first stage of change—***sufficiently unhappy with his current state***. Using Kuhn's model, there have been a lot of anomalies building up in the current paradigm. The industry is changing; his hours are getting cut back. Expenses are rising. If Stuart doesn't do something to change his situation, chaos will eventually ensue. Stuart might get laid off. The company could go bankrupt. Stuart has to be aware enough that the anomalies are starting to grow and be unhappy enough to be motivated to change.

But, what can he do? He can't afford to just quit his job. His belief that there's nothing he can do is a resisting force. He's been frozen in a job that doesn't support his family. But unless he unfreezes those resisting forces, things are likely to get worse.

That night, Stu talks to his wife about the problem. She says, "Remember when we first met? You had dreams of being a writer. You are a REALLY good writer. And I know for a fact you have at least three unfinished pieces. What if you started freelance writing to bring in some extra money?"

Suddenly, Stu was in the second phase of change—***believing that he is capable of making the change***.

He thinks it's a great idea and feels excited and energized. But, how can he do it? How can he start writing again after all these years?

The next day at work, Stu mentions his idea to his boss. "Why don't you contact some of those book reps that are always stopping in here? See what they think."

Stuart has now moved into the third phase of change—***knowing what to do to achieve the goal***. The strength of the driving forces is starting to grow now, and the equilibrium is shifting.

The next day, Stuart calls the book reps that he's gotten to know over the years, and pitches his ideas to them. Of course, as happens in publishing, you can't just make one call and land a book deal. It takes concerted, repeated effort. In other words, Stuart has to enter the fourth stage of change—***building your goal into your daily life***. Every day, before going to work, Stuart makes calls, asks for referrals, sends in sample chapters, and finishes writing his books.

After a few weeks, his goal is achieved! Stuart gets a publishing deal! Now it's time to "refreeze" and create new equilibrium. He wants to continue to grow his relationship with his new publisher. After all, what good is change if it doesn't last?

Essentially, Lewin says to "refreeze" and prevent things from going back to the original unpleasant state. For example, you hate your life, you sit around watching TV, you get up off the couch (unfreeze), apply for a new job, get the new job, and then get rid of the couch and all the other stuff that kept you in that earlier state of affairs (refreeze), so that your new job doesn't take you back to hating your life. Lewin is telling us, as former

CEO of General Electric Jack Welch did, to "Change before you have to." Lewin tells us how.

In the next chapter, we'll look at some of the factors that can help personal and professional change stick around long enough to become the "current paradigm."

# CHAPTER FIVE

# The Four Keys to Lasting Change

*"All meaningful and lasting change starts first in your imagination and then works its way out."*

–Albert Einstein

Will is the Sales Director of a medium sized real estate firm. The firm was actually started by Will's grandfather, who passed it on to his dad, who is passing it on to Will next year. Because the business has been in the family so long, the team is kind of "stuck" in the old way of doing things.

Will wants the team to grow so he brought in a bunch of new technology, such as a cloud-based platform for managing the paperwork, text-message direct sales marketing, the use of animated YouTube videos, live streaming from Open Houses, and other innovations.

Unfortunately, while his team wants to change, they're not using the new technology. In order for Will to help his team grow, he's going to need to use one of the core concepts in psychology, Operant Conditioning.

## Bring in the Reinforcements

When a person wants to affect behavior, one way to do it us through the use of Operant Conditioning. This concept popularized by B. F. Skinner, is the process of applying the law of effect to control behavior by manipulating its consequences. There are four operant conditioning strategies that are the keys to lasting change: Positive Reinforcement, Negative Reinforcement, Punishment, and Extinction.

- **Positive reinforcement** strengthens or increases the frequency of a desirable behavior by making a pleasant consequence contingent on its occurrence.

- **Negative reinforcement** strengthens or increases the frequency of a desirable behavior by making the avoidance of an unpleasant consequence contingent on its occurrence.

- **Punishment** eliminates or decreases an undesirable behavior by making an unpleasant consequence contingent on its occurrence.

- **Extinction** eliminates or decreases an undesirable behavior by making the removal of a pleasant consequence contingent on occurrence.

So, in the case of Will, he decides to use one of these techniques on each of his employees.

With Tina, Will uses positive reinforcement. When she uses one of the new technologies, Will praises her. After two weeks of consistently using the new technology, Tina gets a Starbucks gift card.

With Bruce, Will uses negative reinforcement. Every time Will uses the new technology, he gets to skip the daily briefing meeting that everyone hates going to.

With Shelly, Will uses punishment every time she uses the old system. Every time she "forgets" to use the cloud-based platform, for example, and prints the papers out instead, Shelly has to donate $5 to the printer ink fund.

And, finally, Will uses the concept of extinction with Roger. First, he lets Roger have first pick of the listings for a week. But, then he tells Roger that if he doesn't start using the new technology, he'll lose the privilege of first choice.

Another concept that Will can use is the idea of shaping. **Shaping** is the creation of a new behavior by the positive reinforcement of successive approximations of the desired behavior. So, in order to get Peggy to start using the new technologies, he uses positive reinforcement whenever she uses ONE of them. Then, two of them. Eventually he only reinforces her if she uses all of them.

The most common of the four are positive reinforcements and punishment.

## Viva Las Vegas

What's interesting, though, is that Will can also offer the reinforcements on a different schedule to get different outcomes.

Schedules of Reinforcement:

- A **continuous reinforcement schedule** administers a reward each time a desired behavior occurs.
- An **intermittent reinforcement schedule** rewards behavior only periodically.

If you've ever been to Las Vegas, and gambled in the casinos, you've experienced intermittent reinforcement and probably discovered how powerfully motivating it is. You put a quarter in the machine (or your casino card, these days), and play a game. Sometimes you win, sometimes you lose. When you win, the amount varies. Sometimes it's a small amount and sometimes it's a huge amount. The casinos don't give out huge amounts every time. Instead they reinforce your behavior by only offering wins a certain percentage of the time, and only offering large prizes infrequently.

---

*Continuous reinforcement will draw forth a desired behavior through shaping.*

*Intermittent reinforcement will maintain the desired behavior.*

---

## Using Positive Reinforcement

There are two laws that affect how well reinforcement works.

1. *Law of contingent reinforcement*—For a reward to have maximum reinforcing value, it must be delivered only if the desired behavior is exhibited.
2. *Law of immediate reinforcement*—The more immediate the delivery of a reward after the occurrence of a desirable behavior, the greater the reinforcing value of the reward.

## To use Positive Reinforcement

- Clearly identify desired behaviors.
- Maintain a diverse inventory of rewards.
- Inform everyone what must be done to get rewards.
- Recognize individual differences when allocating rewards.
- Follow the laws of immediate and contingent reinforcement.

## Using Punishment

Clearly, positive reinforcement is a better option than punishment. But if you've tried rewards and they aren't working, and you really need the person to change, punishment is an effective technique.

In the workplace, to punish an employee, a manager may deny the person a valued reward (such as verbal praise or pay) or the manager may administer an unpleasant outcome (such as a verbal reprimand, pay reduction, or demotion). To be fair and effective in using punishment, you should do the following:

- Tell the person what is being done wrong.
- Tell the person what is being done right.
- Make sure the punishment matches the behavior.
- Administer the punishment in private.
- Follow the laws of immediate and contingent reinforcement.

## Using Operant Conditioning on Your Goals

So, how can you use these ideas to make sure that you "freeze" the new state and ensure that you continue to engage in the behaviors that lead to the accomplishment of your goals? By setting up a system of positive reinforcement (or punishment, if needed) for yourself.

One example relates to weight loss. There are several online programs where a person who desires to lose weight can "bet" a certain amount of money that they will lose a specified amount of weight within a period of time. If they lose the weight, they get additional money—either a portion of the pot or a matched amount to their original bet. So, if Jenny wants to lose twenty-five pounds, she puts in $100, and bets that she can lose the weight in four months. If she does, she gets $1,000. If she doesn't, she loses the $100. This is both positive reinforcement and punishment.

As we've learned, though, it would be even more effective if the reinforcement were intermittent. So, for every five pounds, or a random interval, Jenny were to get a financial reward, she would be far more likely to stick to her weight loss plan than if she has to wait until the end to get the reward.

We will get more into developing rewards for your goals in a later section of the book. The operant conditioning techniques we've mentioned are all designed to influence one's behavior, not the underlying attitude.

To shape attitude, we can look at a classic motivation concept used in advertising called Balance Theory.

## Heider's Balance Theory

In the psychology of motivation, balance theory is a theory of attitude change, proposed by Fritz Heider, who said that we are motivated by things in order to achieve psychological balance, consistently over time. So, in order for you to be motivated and have a positive attitude about something, it has to be consistent with your underlying mindset.

For example, let's say that you and your friend want to go out to lunch. He suggests a sandwich shop that you refuse to patronize because the owners of the shop are big game sport hunters. You dislike the shop, but you like your friend. There is an imbalance there. Depending on which is stronger, your opinion of the sandwich shop will likely change, or your opinion of your friend will change. It's either, "Maybe it doesn't make a difference if I eat there or not. The owner's personal lives don't make a difference in the company," or "I can't believe he is willing to support a company like that!"

Here's a way of looking at it, visually. P is Person One. X is Person Two, and O is the sandwich company.

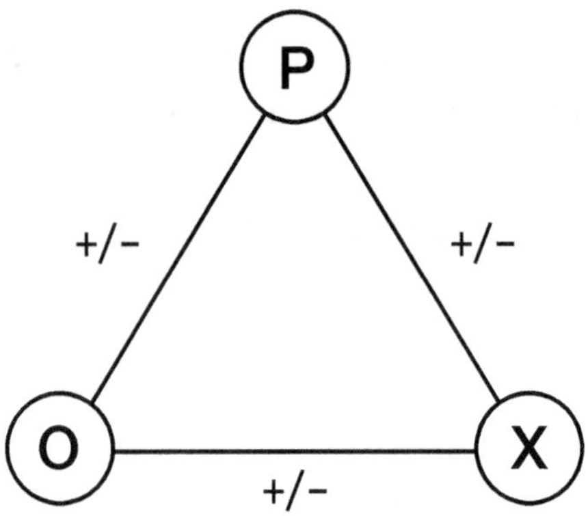


Cognitive balance is achieved when there are three positive links or two negatives with one positive. Everyone likes each other and the sandwich company, or the two people both agree that the sandwich company is bad.

Two positive links and one negative link creates imbalance or Cognitive Dissonance. If you don't like the sandwich company and your friend does, you have to

Decide that O isn't so bad after all,

Decide that X isn't as great as originally thought, or

Conclude that X couldn't really have known about the history of O.

Any of these will result in psychological balance, thus resolving the dilemma and satisfying the drive.

(Person P could also avoid object X and other person O entirely, lessening the stress created by psychological imbalance.)

In order to use balance theory to create lasting change, you've got to make sure that your attitudes toward the objects of change are consistent. Here is an example.

## Chris and the Dating Dilemma

Chris wants to settle down and get married again. She had one failed marriage, and her ex-husband ran off with a younger woman, leaving her alone to raise their two young sons. Her kids are now gone off to college, and she hates the idea of dating. But in order to find a husband, she's going to have to date. So she starts dating, but has a negative attitude about it.

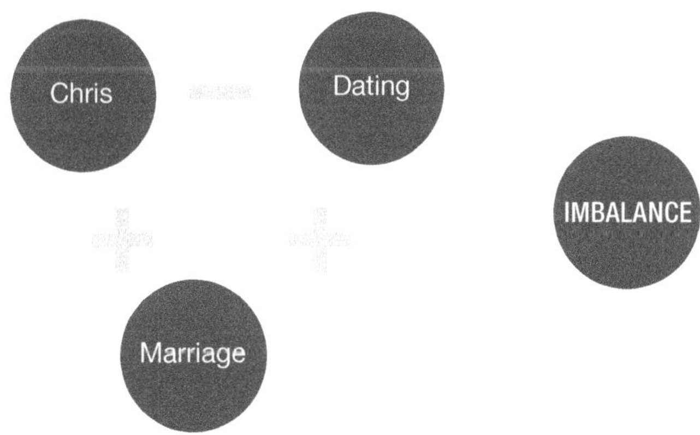


Because this is an imbalanced scenario, Chris likes marriage but hates dating, but dating leads to marriage, she is going to either have to change her attitude about dating, or decide that dating isn't an important part of getting married.

If she doesn't change her attitude about either dating or marriage, she is unlikely to succeed in her goal of getting married. She'll either sabotage dates by choosing the wrong kind of men, canceling the dates at the last minute, or some other behavior that is consistent with her underlying attitude that "dating sucks."

Say that Chris changes her attitude about dating. She uses the idea of positive reinforcement and rewards herself with a mani-pedi after every date. Soon, she starts to have a positive attitude about the dating process because she associates it with something fun.

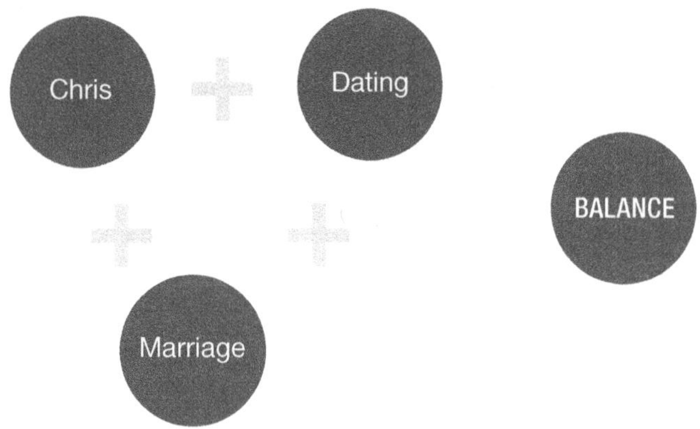


Or, maybe she decides she doesn't want to get married again, after all. This is her time to explore life, travel, and make new friends. She changes her attitude about marriage by associating it with the punishing things her ex-husband did.

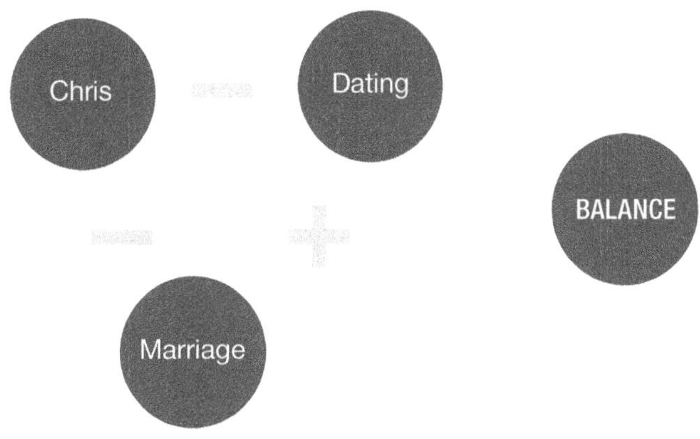


Regardless, Chris has to have Cognitive Balance in order for her to achieve her goal.

## Using Balance Theory to Create Your Own Lasting Change

In order for you to use balance theory to create your own lasting changes in personal or professional growth, you've got to look at your underlying attitude or framework and identify if you have cognitive balance or dissonance.

### WEIGHT LOSS

You want to lose weight but you don't want to stop drinking wine and eating chocolate. You can either decide it's not worth it to drink wine and eat chocolate, stop trying to lose weight, or find a plan that lets you lose weight and still consume chocolate and wine.

### CAREER

You want to get a promotion but don't want to manage people, and the new job is a management position. You can either not go for the promotion, change your attitude about managing people, or find a way to take the promotion and not have to manage people.

### MONEY

You want to save a million dollars but live in a really expensive city. You can either give up the idea of saving a million dollars, move to a less expensive city, or find a way to save a million dollars (maybe slowly) while living in an expensive city.

In Part One of GROW! We looked at the foundations for personal and professional growth. Now it's time to apply what you've learned, and discover the GROW! System for Change.

---

*What is your heart calling you to do? Whatever it is, you've already got what it takes inside you right now.*

---

# Part Two

## *The GROW! System for Change*

# CHAPTER SIX
# G: Goals

*"To live a fulfilled life, we need to keep creating the "what is next," of our lives. Without dreams and goals there is no living, only merely existing, and that is not why we are here."*

—Mark Twain

## About the GROW! System

Congratulations! You have now laid the rich soil that will fertilize the seeds of your present life so that they can grow into the life of your dreams.

Part Two of this book will get into the "how" in personal and professional growth. As we mentioned in the Introduction, GROW is an acronym that stands for Goals, Realign, Overcome obstacles, and Work. Each of these letters represents a chapter in the second part of the book. First, you need to set goals, then you need to realign your mind and actions to be consistent with those goals, overcome the internal and external obstacles that come up, and then "work" the plan. By the end of this section, you'll have the ideas and concepts you need to form a fully executable plan in Section Three.

In this chapter, we'll cover the G in GROW, which is Goals. In order to set effective goals, we need to engage in some "pre-goal setting" activities.

## Pre-Goal Setting: The Four S's

Cathy was driving home from WalMart with some groceries to make dinner for her son, who was home from college for spring break. Frustrated, she looked around and thought, I'm 57 and driving an old car. I'll probably never own my own house. I'm job hunting. It seems like 62 is creeping up on me too fast. I want to find my passion in life, but it's frustrating to still be searching.

Before Cathy can set goals for her life, it's necessary for her to do some Pre-Goal Setting. There are four pillars to Pre Goal Setting.

### • PILLAR ONE: SELF-ACCEPTANCE

First you must accept yourself and your desire to grow and improve.

HOW TO: Write down accomplishments from your professional life as motivation to keep achieving. Remember, there is more you can accomplish when you put your mind to it.

Cathy is a successful accountant with a lot of career accomplishments. In addition, she's raised her children alone, with no financial or emotional support from their father. And, she proudly notes, both of them are doing well in college and are fine young men. Looking back like this helps Cathy to see that she is the kind of person who will ALWAYS want to grow and improve. Just because she feels like she is "searching," doesn't mean she hasn't already accomplished a lot.

• PILLAR TWO: SELF-RESPECT

We often need reminding that we already have the skills and qualities to reach our goals.

HOW TO: Take time to reflect on what you are most proud of about yourself. Write down the positive qualities, characteristics, and traits that you possess.

Cathy makes a list of her positive qualities. Because she is modest, she feels funny writing things down, so she imagines that her sister is telling them to her. Cathy's sister would say that she is intelligent, brave, resilient, adventurous, fun, hard working, flexible, and independent. So, Cathy writes those things down to remind herself that she does have the qualities she needs to succeed in life.

• PILLAR THREE: SELF-CONFIDENCE

During a struggle, it is easy to forget our past accomplishments.

HOW TO: Write down situations when you used your positive qualities. This will help you build confidence and resilience.

This exercise was pretty easy for Cathy. She remembers (and writes down) times when life challenged her. There was the time when she was fired. The time when her mother-in-law tried to steal money from her. There was the time when she found out the man she was dating had another girlfriend the whole time. But instead of just remembering the challenges, Cathy then wrote down which of the positive qualities from Pillar Two she used in each situation.

- PILLAR FOUR: SELF DIRECTION

Think about the areas where you need most improvement, such as time management or taking initiative.

HOW TO: What changes do you need to make? Write them down.

Cathy completes the Rate Your Life questionnaire at the end of this chapter, and gets some clarity on exactly what areas in her life she would like to grow.

## Vision

Another important step to take before setting goals is to establish a vision. Many people think that a "vision statement" is something that only companies use. Not true at all! Look at it this way, if you were going to take a car trip, you wouldn't just get in the car and start driving. You'd establish a destination first. "I want to go to Los Angeles." That's your goal. But, you need to have a vision for both the trip and what it's going to be like when you get to Los Angeles. There are many routes to take. Some are fast and expedient. Others are more scenic. Do you want to take a week or a month? Are you going to drive a sports car or an SUV? All of these factors will influence your getting to Los Angeles, and you need to plan them before you ever get in the car, or else you risk not getting to your destination.

## The Three Ps of a Powerful Vision

Here are three tips on how to set a powerful vision.

1. *Present tense,* as though we have already achieved our vision.

2. *Powerful language,* using motivating words and concepts.

3. *Positive outcomes,* avoiding qualifiers like "if, could, might . . ." and relating what will be happening rather than what we won't be doing. For example, "I have stopped . . ." is not a positive outcome

Here is Cathy's Vision Statement.

> I am living a life of passion and purpose. I use my talents and skills both at work and in my personal life, and I am fulfilled. At work, I know that I deserve "a place at the table" with the movers and shakers in the organization. I am respected for

> my knowledge and for the quality of work that I do, and I am paid well for it. In my personal life, my children respect me and consider me to be a role model for the kind of woman they'd want to marry. I have an intimate relationship with a life partner who is worthy of my loyalty and support. I have a lot to offer in all of my relationships, and I choose people who are grateful to have me in their lives.

## Translate Your Vision into Goals

Although it's important to have a powerful vision, a vision isn't going to change your life. It's too lofty and not specific enough. You need to be able to translate those visions into actual goals. But, goal setting isn't as easy as saying, "I'm going to change my life for the better."

## The Problem with Goal Setting

The problem with goal setting that crops up most often is confusing the plan with the execution. This was very clearly described by W. Edwards Deming, the legendary management theorist who helped create the spectacular success of the Japanese car industry. It's a story that's often been told. Deming was shunned by American automakers because his strategies were so unconventional.

He wasn't against goal setting, but he felt it had to be done with great care. Otherwise people would just start cutting corners in order to meet challenging goals. There's also the flip side of this: the danger of setting too many goals, or goals that are too easy, so they can all be attained. Even the process of goal setting can be self-sabotaging. An individual or an organization can spend so much time setting perfectly calibrated goals that the time for achieving them becomes limited.

---

*The problem with goal setting that crops up most often is confusing the plan with the execution.*

---

Suppose you have a goal of closing ten sales every month. If that's too little, you may be tempted to coast during the later part of a month once you've achieved the relatively easy goal. Or if the expectations are too high, you might feel compelled to make too many presentations and not give buyers the individual attention they deserve.

Goal setting is a positive and powerful practice when it tells you where you are and where you're going. **Effective goal setting shows what success will require during the journey and what it will look like upon arrival.** When practiced poorly, however, goal setting can negatively impact your work and the profitability of your organization.

## Write Your Goals Down!

Studies have shown only three percent of the population engage in some form of goal setting and only one percent actually write them down.

And here's an interesting coincidence. **The one percent of the population that writes goals down is just about the same number as the highest achieving, highest income-earning men and women throughout the country.**

There's a strong inference, therefore, that setting goals is the genesis from which all great things can be accomplished—and certainly great things from a financial perspective. Read any book on achievement or personal development and the message will be right there on the page. Goals equal success.

Whenever we speak of goals, we will be referring to goals that are written down. If they're not written, they're not goals. They're dreams, or they're wishes. Unwritten goals can't be achieved because they aren't goals to begin with. On the other hand, written goals have a fighting chance—simply because of the fact that they've been put in writing.

---

*Unwritten goals can't be achieved because they aren't goals to begin with. They're dreams, or they're wishes.*

---

## Why Are Written Goals Important?

When you write anything down, even a shopping list, you do so because you expect to read it at some point in the future. Writing something now implies reading it—and perhaps living it—at some future time. When you write down a goal, you automatically become a future-oriented individual.

And something else happens too. Since we go to the trouble of writing goals because we want to achieve them, there's another automatic psychological result. You become a motivated and actively success oriented human being. You're not only a believer in the future. You're also a believer in your success in the future.

It's so simple. Not necessarily easy, but definitely simple. Write down your goals, review them on a regular basis, and keep them fresh, clear, and specific in your mind.

## Get SMART

Effective goal setting means defining objectives in practical, measurable terms. You also need to identify the resources, time and funds you'll need to attain them. Once you know where you want to go and you feel confident you have the means to get there, the next step is to put this all into action. This is why so many people use the system that's known by the acronym SMART. The SMART system is simple, down-to-earth and gets the job done. Now, each goal must be defined so that it meets the following criteria:

**S—for specific.** Effective goals are well-defined and focused. For example, "Obtain a new billion dollar corporate client in the Boston property insurance market" is more specific than "Get more business." A highly specific goal becomes a magnet, pulling you and your resources toward it. The more focused your energies, the more power you generate.

**M—for measurable.** Frame your goals in such a way that you can measure your progress. For example, plan on measuring monthly or against last year's figures. A goal without a measurable outcome is like a sports competition without a scoreboard or scorekeeper. Numbers are an essential part of sales. Include numbers in your goals to know if you're on track. A white board posted in your office can help as a daily reminder to keep you focused on the measurable results you want to attain.

When you're working toward a goal, you will also need measurable feedback to determine whether you're succeeding or need to change direction. Feedback, if it's correctly done, can very encouraging and motivating. This also includes feedback from yourself. Again, you must keep close tabs on your progress and respond congruently. Feel good when you've done well. And be aware that negative self-talk is just as demotivating as negative comments from other people.

**A—for attainable.** An ambitious person sometimes sets goals beyond reach. No one has ever built a multi-million-dollar career overnight, or in a month or even in a year. Venture capitalists and angel investors discard countless business plans of companies with outlandish goals. Dream big and aim for the stars but keep one foot firmly based in reality.

**"A" can also stand for actionable.** When you're setting goals, be sure you've developed them from strategic plans to specific actions that can be performed and evaluated. Goals without action plans are just pretty words.

The purpose of goals is to move your life forward. So you need to position the bar very carefully when setting those objectives. If the bar is too high, we set ourselves up for failure and disappointment. In that event, many people will just stop trying.

On the other hand, if the bar is set too low all you have to do is step over it. There's no satisfaction or recognition or genuine accomplishment. A goal has to stretch you in order to be worth doing. Recognize that a goal has to feel worthwhile and set goals that will accomplish a dual purpose. You need to attain them, and you need to feel really good about having done so.

**R—for relevant.** Achievable goals are based on the current conditions and realities of your environment. You may desire to have your best year in sales, for example, or increase your commissions by 50%, but if a recession is looming and three new competitors opened in your market, then your goals aren't relevant to the realities of the market.

People sometimes make the mistake of choosing goals that are without real point or purpose. For instance, you might set a goal to hand out one hundred business cards a month. You might meet that goal, but its relevance to anything else is difficult to measure or establish. To be relevant, a goal has to be profitable in some fashion. That's not to say that every goal has to be measurable in dollars and cents, but it does have to possess a clear advantage or benefit to your life.

**T—for time-specific.** Goals and objectives just don't get done when there's no time frame tied to the goal-setting process. Whether your goal is to increase commissions by 20% or lose 5 pounds, choose a time-frame to accomplish your goal. Give yourself a reasonable time frame for achieving this. Then break it down into smaller, short-term increments. Realistically, you may not achieve a certain percent increase early in the year, but you can still work toward it.

Divide your goal percent increase into monthly or quarterly increments that allow you to build on your momentum. This produces measurable, attainable and short-term goals to pursue.

Now it's time to set those goals! Take the Rate Your Life questionnaire on the following page, and choose some goals to work on. Make sure they are written as SMART goals!

## THE RATE YOUR LIFE QUESTIONNAIRE

1. How would you rate your life out of 10 (10 being you can't imagine it could possibly be any better) in the following areas?

Physical health __________
Money __________
Career/work __________
Hobbies/recreation __________
Marriage/romance __________
Family and friends __________
Spiritual development __________
Charity/Community Service __________
Learning/Intellectual growth __________

2. Given these scores, which 2–3 areas are you willing to improve over the next 6 months to make the biggest difference to your life? (Maximum Three)

Physical health __________
Money __________
Career/work __________
Hobbies/recreation __________
Marriage/romance __________
Family and friends __________
Spiritual development __________
Charity/Community Service __________
Learning/Intellectual growth __________

3. What three things are you most tolerating or putting up with in your life?

   1. ________________________________________
   2. ________________________________________
   3. ________________________________________

4. What three things are you most loving in your life?

   1. ________________________________________
   2. ________________________________________
   3. ________________________________________

5. If you could have more of ONE thing in your life right now, what would it be?

____________________________________________

## CREATE YOUR GOALS

6. Create 2–3 goals which would make a BIG difference to your life. Choose goals which would put a big smile on your face, and be achievable within 6 months.

   1. ________________________________________
   2. ________________________________________
   3. ________________________________________

7. Imagine six months have passed, and you've done it! You have achieved each of these goals. Write down how you would feel having achieved each of these.

Goal #1: ____________________________________

I feel: ______________________________________

____________________________________________

Goal #2: ______________________________

I feel: ______________________________

______________________________

Goal #3: ______________________________

I feel: ______________________________

______________________________

(Hint: If you wouldn't feel wonderful about each of these, then you might like to go back to Step 6. and choose bigger or smarter goals)

# CHAPTER SEVEN
## R: Realign

*"Inaction breeds doubt and fear. Action breeds confidence and courage. If you want to conquer fear, do not sit home and think about it. Go out and get busy."*

—Dale Carnegie

"I'd like to order a double cheeseburger, a large fries, and a soda."

"Will that be all, Ma'am?"

"Actually, add in a large chocolate shake too, please."

Pam knew she shouldn't be at the drive through. She'd been really good on her diet for two weeks, and this extra 45 pounds isn't going to lose itself. *What's wrong with me*, she wondered? *Why do I keep doing this?* Taking the bag, she reaches in and grabs a handful of hot French Fries to eat at she drives away.

* * *

It was the night before Don's interview with the police department. His whole life he'd wanted nothing more than to become a police officer. He'd passed the written test, the physical, and the background check. Now, all that remained was the in-person interview, and he planned to get a good night's sleep so that he could be sharp for it.

"Hey man," Don's best friend George said as he opened the front door. "Let's go get wasted."

"Sorry, I've got that interview tomorrow."

"Dude, you need to blow off some steam. You'll do better if you're not stressed out about it."

Grabbing his coat as he walked out the front door, Don thought, *George is right. What does it matter anyway? I'll probably bomb the interview, so I might as well have some fun.* As he climbs into George's truck to head to the local dive bar, Don feels his emotions begin to sink.

Mary has been divorced for a year now, and is on another first date. It's her fourth one in six months. This time, it's a good looking attorney named Greg. Mary's best friend introduced them at a party last week, and they had a definite connection, so when he called to ask her out, Mary felt hopeful.

Unfortunately, during dinner, Mary couldn't stop talking. She went on and on about her ex-husband and his over-attachment to his mother. She talked about her cat Mr. Goober and how he loves to play with grapes. She even told Greg an embarrassing story from middle school. The whole time she was watching Greg lose interest and thinking, *why can't I shut up? I'm blowing another first date!*

## If Nothing Changes, Nothing Changes

As the scenarios above illustrate, it's not enough to have a goal. No matter how SMART your goal is, if you don't realign your behavior so that you're engaging in activities that will actually lead you to your goal, you won't achieve it. As the old saying goes, if nothing changes, nothing changes.

So, let's take a look at some of the behaviors that may need realigning. In the following spaces, rewrite the goals you chose in Chapter Six. Then, underneath them, write down what you have been doing (or not doing) that has kept you in your current state. After that, identify an action you can take that will be in alignment with your goal.

Goal #1: ______________________________

I'm in this situation because of the following behaviors:

______________________________

______________________________

______________________________

Following are some new behaviors that I can engage in, that will lead me to my goal.

______________________________

______________________________

______________________________

Goal #2: ______________________________

I'm in this situation because of the following behaviors:

______________________________

______________________________

______________________________

Following are some new behaviors that I can engage in, that will lead me to my goal.

______________________________

______________________________

______________________________

Goal #3: ______________________________

I'm in this situation because of the following behaviors:

______________________________

______________________________

______________________________

Following are some new behaviors that I can engage in, that will lead me to my goal.

______________________________

______________________________

______________________________

## What's Holding You Back?

Now that you've identified what you need to do, you should be good to go, right? Not so fast. We are betting that you already knew what you need to be doing to reach your goal. It's not rocket science to understand that to lose weight, you need to stop stuffing your face with chili fries and move your body. To become more organized, you actually have to spend some time cleaning out your closet. It's not magically going to happen by just writing it down. You have to DO the things you need to do. And, chances are, there's a reason you haven't been doing them all along.

*But, you don't understand. I have a lot going on right now. Seriously. There's this project at work, and I'm just getting over the flu. My parents are having problems and my kids are in sports tournaments this month. Once those things change, then I'll do what I know I need to do.*

Sound familiar? As we discussed earlier, there are some times that are better than others to launch a personal or professional growth plan. But, if you are consistently "too busy" to work on your goals, it's time to realign. Either let the goal go for awhile, or let some other things slide for awhile so you can focus on your goals.

Sometimes, it can be hard to see our own behavior clearly. There's a concept called the Johari Window, that helps people better understand their relationship with themselves and others. It was created by psychologists Joseph Luft and Harrington Ingham in 1955, and is named Johari because the men combined their first names.

## The Johari Window

The Johari Window breaks our behavior up into four categories.

| | |
|---|---|
| What We Can See In Ourselves—That Other People Cannot See In Us (Private Self) | What Other People Can See In Us—That We Can See In Ourselves (Public Self) |
| What We Cannot See In Ourselves—That Other People Cannot See In Us (Unknown) | What Other People Can See In Us—That We Cannot See In Ourselves (Blind Side) |

Normally, the Johari Window is used to illustrate personality traits or psychological qualities that can be hidden or revealed. For our purposes, though, we are going to apply the concepts to behaviors that lead to (or away from) personal and professional growth.

In the upper left quadrant of the window is our **Private Self**. These are things that we see in ourselves that other people cannot. It's the late night snacking or the fact that you don't keep a checkbook. These are examples of private things that you do that only you know about.

In the upper right quadrant is our **Public Self**. These are things we see in ourselves that other people see too.

This is when we take selfies of ourselves at the gym, or when we drive a really expensive car.

The lower left quadrant is **Unknown**, and are the things that we can't see in ourselves, and no one else can see them either. This is the area of the greatest potential. It's the area of growth that you, or someone else, BELIEVES you can do, but it's not based on facts or evidence, but on intuition. "I think you would make a good professor."

Finally, the lower right quadrant is our **Blind Side**. This is what other people can see in us that we can't see in ourselves. This goes for both positive and negative behaviors. We all have that person in our lives that we see engaging in a negative behavior and they don't see how it leads to them not achieving their goals. They say, "I am so tired of being broke." Yet, the first time they get a paycheck, they spend it on luxury items. You think to yourself, "If they would just pay down some debt instead of spending money the first minute they get it, they wouldn't be broke all the time."

How can we use the Johari Window to realign our behaviors?

### PRIVATE SELF

In this quadrant, identify the behaviors that you know in your heart of hearts you are doing that need to change. These are the things you do when no one else is looking, and keep you from achieving your goal. Go back and add them to the list of behaviors earlier in the chapter.

## PUBLIC SELF

In this quadrant, identify the things you are doing publicly because you are concerned with status, image, what other people think of you, et cetera, that may not be in alignment with your goals. For example, if you have a goal to spend more time with your children, but find yourself saying yes to volunteering, overtime at work, or other public things that keep you from making time for what matters to you, write them down.

The next two categories are things you can't see in yourself, and so you'll need to get a trusted advisor to help you. Here are some people you can enlist:

**People Who Care**—Who are the nurturers who listen, encourage, support, acknowledge, and emotionally support you?

**People Who Confront**—Who are the truth tellers in your life who care enough to confront you privately when you need to make changes?

**People with Expertise**—Who are the experts you value most on the job, in your profession, and in your areas of interest who help you learn what you need or want to know?

**People with Social Contacts**—Who are the critical hub people who know a vast array of the people you need to know to achieve your goals on and off the job?

**People to Play with**—Who are the people who share your passion and make time to join you in enjoying your interests, hobbies, and activities?

**People Who Feed Your Need for Community**—Who are your soul mates, the ones who share your beliefs and nurture your common values?

### UNKNOWN

For this quadrant, choose a trusted advisor who has already achieved the goal you want to achieve. Ask him or her, "What are some of the things you did to achieve the goal? How did you stop doing the behaviors that weren't in alignment with the goal?" In other words, right now, there are behaviors that you may not know about, and the trusted advisor doesn't know if you do or don't do them. But, asking the questions can reveal otherwise hidden information and ideas.

### BLIND SPOT

Ask your trusted advisor, "What are the things that you see me do that are keeping me from achieving my goals, that I may not be aware of?" For example, if you have a goal to find a meaningful relationship, but only go to bars, your trusted advisor might say, "You are looking in the wrong places to meet men." By the way, it's important to "hear" what the trusted advisor says without being defensive or arguing. Sometimes it's hard to hear negative feedback about our behavior, especially when it's a blind spot that we may be hearing about for the first time.

## The Right Tools for the Job

Now that we know what to do, what not to do, and have some insight into how to realign our behaviors, it's time to make it easier to succeed. Having the right tools can make or break your ability to engage in the behaviors you want. Here's an example.

Terry has a goal that she wants to eat healthier. She wants to eat more steamed vegetables, brown rice, and cook beans from scratch. The thing is, she doesn't do it. Using our Johari Window example, here is what she's doing.

**Private:** Terry procrastinates making the healthy food she wants to be eating because it's time consuming and messy.

**Public:** When she goes out to eat, she always orders the healthy option—salad, steamed vegetables, brown rice, etc.

**Unknown:** She doesn't know what she can be doing differently, and since the other people in her life only see her eating healthfully, they don't either.

**Blind Spot:** Terry's teenage daughter sees that if her mom had better tools to make healthy cooking easier, she would be more inclined to do it.

## Tools for Success

**Healthy cooking**—rice cooker, vegetable steamer, good pots and pans, cookbook.

**Weight loss**—online food tracker, support system, food scale.

**Exercise**—comfortable clothes, good shoes, pedometer, heart rate monitor, exercise equipment.

**Managing your money**—budget software, online banking.

**Saving money**—automatic savings plan.

**Better time management**—a to do list, a good calendar, a system.

Now the thing is, the best tool in the world isn't going to help you if you don't use it. We aren't recommending that you go out and buy a bunch of kitchen gadgets or an expensive treadmill. We are recommending that you ask yourself, "Is there anything that would make this a little easier?" After all, you'll be more likely to actually do something if its easier.

# CHAPTER EIGHT
## O: Overcome Obstacles

*"Success consists of going from failure to failure without loss of enthusiasm."*
—WINSTON CHURCHILL

In 2003, Kris Carr was a 32-year-old New Yorker just enjoying life. But then, a regular checkup at her doctor's office changed everything.

> "On Valentine's Day in 2003, I was diagnosed with a rare and incurable (yet thankfully slow-growing) stage IV cancer. This WTF moment sparked a deep desire in me to stop holding back and start participating in my well-being. Though I can't be cured, I can still be healthy—I can still feel better, love harder and have a more joyful life. So I hit the road on a self-care pilgrimage and haven't looked back. More than a decade

> later, my life is more connected and magical than it was before my diagnosis. Although I still have cancer, I am healthy, and I run a mission-driven business that serves my community and makes me feel profoundly grateful each and every day. If I can pull that off, just imagine what YOU can do."*

Kris created a series of successful self-help books and documentaries. Eventually, she launched her own wellness website, which is followed by more than 40,000 people. Today, she is celebrating a decade of "thriving with cancer," and is now revered as one of the most prominent experts on healthy living.

## There Will Be Obstacles

As you are moving forward in the GROW! System for Change, it's not a matter of IF there will be obstacles, it's a matter of WHEN they will appear, and how you will handle them when they do.

You'll remember Lewin's Equation, "Behavior is a function of the Person and the Environment." There are two types of obstacles we'll address in this chapter. Obstacles that are internal to the person (thoughts and attitudes), and obstacles that are external in the environment (other people, unexpected situations).

---

* http://kriscarr.com/meet-kris/

## Internal Obstacles

Whenever we launch a change, whether it's positive or challenging, there are a series of negative emotions that we go through.

FIVE NEGATIVE EMOTIONS OF CHANGE

1. Depression/Frustration/Anger
2. Resolve/Excitement/Elation
3. The Letdown/Blues
4. Impatience/Frustration
5. Sadness/Fear of the Future

Here's how it works.

First, Depression/Frustration/Anger leads you to want to make the change.

Then you feel Resolve/Excitement/Elation as you start.

But then comes the "Blues" or a letdown as you realize that the changes you're making aren't all easy. "This isn't going to be as easy as I thought."

You start to feel Impatience/Frustration at how long it's taking: "When I am going to get there?"

Finally, as the change starts to settle in, there is often a level of Sadness at letting go of the past/Fear of the future.

Here's an example.

Joey is sick of his job working in a gym. The pay is really low and he is at the mercy of the rules set by the gym. He really wants to become a physical therapist. This is step one, Depression/Frustration/Anger.

He enrolls in night school so that he can get his Bachelor's degree in kinesiology. He is determined to get the degree, and get a job as a physical therapist. He's totally excited to go back to school! He's in step two, Resolve/Excitement/Elation.

Things are going well, but he's started to get frustrated. He misses his friends and family, because he's either in school or studying all of the time. And, he is finding that the exams are harder than he thought they would be. He's in step three The Letdown/Blues.

Months go by, and he's taking his classes. But he is still attending lower-level courses, such as History and English. It's getting frustrating. He wants to get on with it, so he can start taking the interesting classes, and graduate! He's in step four. Impatience/Frustration.

Finally, he's done it! It's graduation time, and Joey has lined up a job working at a physical therapy clinic. On the way to give notice at the gym. Joey starts to feel a twinge of sadness and even some fear about the future. "What if I hate it?" Joey is in step five, Sadness/Fear of the Future.

Even when we are making progress toward a goal that we really want, and feel a sense of pride and elation as we accomplish goals, there are always negative emotions that come up at the same time. Here are some tips for handling those emotional obstacles.

1. Understand that these emotions are a normal part of the change process.
2. Pay attention to your emotions. A lot of times your first sign that you're having a deep emotion is behavior. Eating, drinking, shopping, crying a lot. Hurting yourself. Getting sick. Getting in trouble at work or school . . . You wonder "what is wrong with me?" Sabotaging your plan is a good indicator that you have emotions you haven't dealt with.
3. Be kind to yourself. Note, this doesn't mean allow yourself to engage in unhealthy behaviors.
4. Look for small successes.
5. Visualize the positive in the change.

---

*All changes, even the most longed for, have their melancholy; for what we leave behind us is a part of ourselves; we must die to one life before we can enter another.*

—Anatole France

---

## Self-Defeating Thought Patterns

In addition to the emotional obstacles that we face, there are also thought patterns that can become obstacles. Here are several examples of self-defeating thought patterns.

### EXTREME THINKING

Also known as "all or nothing" thinking, this is when we can't see a middle ground. You make one mistake and think, "I am a total failure, I might as well give up."

### IMMINENT DISASTER

This is when you are always waiting for the "other shoe to drop" and for disaster to strike. When things are going well, you think, "This won't last. Eventually something bad will happen." Or you encounter a small obstacle and think, "This is a disaster."

### MAGNIFICATION OF THE NEGATIVE

Similarly, Magnification of the Negative is when you discount your positive accomplishments and overemphasize the negative. "I know I had the best sales record last month, but I came in third this month, so I must be a horrible sales person."

### DIFFICULTY ACCEPTING COMPLIMENTS

This is one that many, many people have. When a person gives you a compliment, do you minimize it, decline the offer of praise, and reinforce your negative thinking? "You liked the presentation? I thought it was too long and I kept reading from my notes. I think I bombed it!"

### OVEREMPHASIS ON "SHOULD" STATEMENTS

This is when we use the idea that something "should" be happening other than the way it is and then use that thought to think negatively about ourselves. "I am 57 years old. I should be more successful by now."

In fact, the "should" statements often reflect underlying attachments and expectations that can lead to negative thought patterns. Here are five categories of thoughts that can trigger self-defeating thought patterns.

## Five Categories that Trigger Self-Defeating Thoughts

### 1. ATTACHMENT TO THINGS

When we find ourselves attached to material things, and we lose them, we can be triggered into feeling badly about ourselves. "I can't believe I had a car accident. I am a terrible driver, and I don't deserve to have nice things." This can lead to Magnification of the Negative.

### 2. EXPECTATIONS OF OTHERS

This is when we have expectations that other people will either agree with you/share your values or that they'll do what you want them to do/think they should do. Then, when they don't, we get into "should" statements. "My boss should stand up for me in front of clients!!"

### 3. EXPECTATIONS OF YOURSELF

This is when we have expectations that we'll think or behave in a certain way. "I should have. . . ." "I never should have" "When I . . ." This can lead to Extreme Thinking.

### 4. ATTACHMENT TO A DIFFERENT TIME

Whether it's the past or the future, sometimes we get attached to a time that isn't the present. We compare things to the way they used to be. "Back in college, I was running ten miles a day." We compare things to the future. "When I finally get some money, we are going to move out of this neighborhood and into someplace nice." When we do this, though, we trigger the "should" thoughts. We think we "should" be like we were in the past, or that we "should" be at our goal already.

### 5. THE IDEA THAT THINGS SHOULD BE DIFFERENT THAN THEY ARE.

Similarly, comparing things as they are now to the way things are for someone else. If you aren't happy with the car you drive, and your friend buys a new Jaguar, and you are focused on the idea that you should have a nice car too, you'll likely trigger a negative thought pattern. "I think your car is great! It gets great gas mileage and your monthly payments are low." "My car sucks. I don't want to be driving this, I want a NICE car like yours."

## Overcoming Mental and Emotional Obstacles

Here are four techniques you can use to overcome mental and emotional obstacles. They are: *evidence, alternatives, implications,* and *usefulness.*

*Evidence.* The most convincing way to confront a nonproductive belief is to show that it is *factually incorrect.*

*Alternative Explanations.* You look for less self-destructive explanations to the cause of the adversity that helps you bounce back. Most events have multiple possible causes. Pessimists have a way of latching onto the worst possible explanations for events—the most permanent, pervasive, and personal ones that make bouncing back even more difficult.

*Implications* for any *Adversity*—Don't make any disaster or misfortune worse than it is. Instead of assuming *the worst consequences,* take a realistic look at *the most likely consequences* to your setback.

*Usefulness* is considering if it's even worth taking time to deal with it—Will worry work? Worry can exact a price that is sometimes worse than adversity itself.

Here's a script you can use to change your thoughts and emotions.

SELF-CORRECTION SCRIPT:

**Start with an *Affirmation*:** "This isn't like me. Normally, I am. . . ."

**Identify what you specifically did that contributed to the problem or failure:** "I didn't like the way I . . ." Be specific.

**Take responsibility by specifying what you can do to rectify the problem:** "To take responsibility, I will . . ." Be specific.

**Focus on the future on how to handle a similar situation next time:** "Next time this happens, I will . . ." Be specific.

## External Obstacles

Sometimes, the obstacles we face aren't inside our heads, but are in the environment. This section will talk about how to overcome those obstacles that are outside ourselves.

There is a Chinese Proverb that goes something like this . . .

> A farmer and his son had a beloved stallion who helped the family earn a living. One day, the farmer's son accidentally left the gate open, and the stallion ran away.
>
> His neighbors exclaimed, "Oh no! Your horse ran away, what terrible luck!" The farmer replied, "Maybe so, maybe not. We'll see."
>
> The horse was running over the hills and through the valleys when he came upon a group of wild stallions. He had the best time running with them. But, one day, they ran past the farmer's ranch, and the horse started missing the comfort of his barn stall. He ran home, and the other stallions were so curious, they followed.
>
> The neighbors shouted out, "Your horse has returned, and brought several horses home with him. What great luck!" The farmer replied, "Maybe so, maybe not. We'll see."
>
> Later that week, the farmer's son was trying to break one of the mares and she threw him to the ground, breaking his leg. The villagers cried,

> "Your son broke his leg, what terrible luck!" The farmer replied, "Maybe so, maybe not. We'll see."
>
> A few weeks later, soldiers from the national army marched through town, recruiting all the able-bodied boys for the army. They did not take the farmer's son, still recovering from his injury. Friends shouted, "Your boy is spared, what tremendous luck!" To which the farmer replied, "Maybe so, maybe not. We'll see."

The moral of the story is that events that happen in our external environment are just that—events. They aren't "good" or "bad" until we label them as such. And, often the thing that looks like a terrible obstacle to our success is simply a stepping stone to something better.

## The Three Umpires

There is another old story about three baseball umpires who are sitting around after a game, talking about the difficulty in making calls.

The first umpire states quite confidently, "If it's a ball, I call it a ball. And if it's a strike I call it a strike."

The second umpire counters, "It isn't that simple or easy, judgment is involved, sometimes it isn't that clear. If it looks like a ball, I call it a ball. If it seems like a strike, I call it a strike."

The third umpire chuckles. "You guys miss the point. It isn't a ball until I call it a ball; and it isn't a strike until I call it a strike."

The first umpire claims we perceive the world as it actually exists. The second umpire claims we interpret the world that exists. The third claims we create the world through our perception of it.

In order to overcome obstacles in our external environment, we need to be like the farmer, and the third umpire. We need to understand that nothing is good or bad until we CALL it good or bad, and instead have the patience to persevere along our chosen course of action.

# CHAPTER NINE
# W: Work

*"Success isn't always about greatness. It's about consistency. Consistent hard work leads to success. Greatness will come."*

—Dwayne "The Rock" Johnson

We've come to the most important part of the GROW! System for Success. Work. As anyone who has ever achieved a goal can tell you, success does not come without work. You can't become a professional or Olympic athlete without spending hours and hours training. You can't start a multi-million dollar company without a dedicated team and many sleepless nights.

There's an old adage that says, "If you want something you don't have, you're going to have to start doing things you don't do."

The key to success in GROW! is to set up a master system where everything you need to do is in one comprehensive plan. It has to encompass time management, physical fitness, a support system, and a strategy for staying inspired when motivation wanes. We've created one, called The Productivity Accelerator, and you'll find it at the end of this chapter. But first, let's look more closely at the core components of success.

---

*"A dream does not become reality through magic; it takes sweat, determination and hard work."*
—Colin Powell

---

## Time Management

Time management is all about focusing your time on what's important. Here are some tips for managing your time effectively.

*Establish your priorities and be ruthless in focusing on them.* If you get an interruption, make a choice—is it more important to continue what I'm doing or is the interruption more important?

*Don't duck the difficult problems or your important work.* We sometimes worry that we can't complete an important task so we try to "get a few things out of the way." But an hour moving forward an important project is far better than getting twenty less important items off your list.

*Establish deadlines.* If something doesn't have a deadline, it doesn't get done. In moderation, pressure motivates.

*Use Your Calendar.* Your calendar is your creed; it establishes what's really important in your life and drives your actions. Set appointments, make commitments, write them out and keep your goals visible.

*Break larger tasks down.* People get stuck with large tasks because they appear too huge to tackle in a reasonable time frame. They keep putting it off. The answer to this problem is to break all large or difficult tasks into their smaller subparts. Then, you can do each of the subparts of the larger project over a series of days.

*Delegate when you can.* Life today is about teams, collaboration, and delegation. We don't do everything ourselves. Using other people's skills and time resources is sometimes the best choice you can make.

## How to Have the Energy You Need to Succeed

As we mentioned earlier, in order for you to be able to accomplish your goals, you'll need to incorporate health-giving activities into your day. This isn't to say you need to wait until you're in peak physical condition before you start to grow. The more you make healthy lifestyle choices, the more energy you'll have to engage in the behaviors you need to be doing in order to succeed. Here are some energy-giving tips.

- Get adequate sleep.
- Limit alcohol consumption.
- Stop smoking.
- Eat less.
- Exercise more.

- Building good eating habits is not about having to eat what you hate. It's about learning to love what's good for you.
- Make small changes. Experiment with new recipes.
- Keep treats out of the home.
- Get a habit of using a smaller plate at home with smaller portions. Eat slowly, and you will soon feel full after eating much less food.
- Get together with friends who like the same exercise so that on the days when you just don't feel like it, they'll help pull you along.
- Join an age and health appropriate team in a sport you enjoy. Winning and losing together with teammates is an easy way to sneak in increased activity.
- At half time, instead of watching commercials and updates, exercise instead of snacking. Let your TV take you and your family members through your paces for fun and health.
- Ride your bike or walk to your local store rather than driving your car.
- Take the stairs instead of the elevator.
- Walk your pets regularly. They'll love it *and* love you more.

## Support Systems for Success

Another important factor in success is having a support system of other people. In an earlier chapter, we explored the idea of Trusted Advisors. It's also a good idea to have role models, mentors, along with your Trusted Advisors.

## Role Model versus Mentor

Many people confuse having a role model with having a mentor. Knowing the difference is critical. While role models are important, they are generally examples rather than teachers. Sports figures, business leaders and celebrities may be great examples as role models, yet unless you have an ongoing, personal relationship with that individual, the impact they will have on your long-term development will be minimal. Basically, a role model is someone you look up to, whereas a mentor is someone who knows you, and helps raise you to their level of success.

### WHAT IS A MENTOR?

There are different kinds of mentors and several definitions of what a mentor actually provides. The specific duties or actions of each mentor will vary according to the specific outcomes you seek. The following is a general definition:

---

*A mentor is a trusted, knowledgeable, experienced individual with a vested interest in assisting those that they mentor in reaching higher levels of accomplishment in their chosen endeavor.*

---

The mentor's role is to teach, coach, and guide those they mentor with integrity, compassion and unrelenting care. The role is also to advise in accomplishing their student's outcomes, goals and desires as agreed upon by the mentor and the student. The mentor also builds trust and passionate determination, inspires and empowers others, and transfers wisdom and experience into the mind, body and spirit. Through all of this, the mentor is able to compress the time table of accomplishment so that the one who is being mentored achieves a higher level of success, faster than he or she would have on their own. Simply put, having a mentor speeds up your success.

## Checklist for Choosing the Right Mentor

✓ Chose a mentor with an outstanding track record in the field you wish to conquer. Look for testimonials and success stories of their existing or prior students. If the individual is advertising to mentor, they won't mind that you seek references. Sometimes, the students do not wish to be made public, but in most cases the satisfied student is pleased to be able to refer the mentor that made such a difference in their life.

✓ Find the best. You deserve the best that life has to offer, so seek the best in your field and be fearless in approaching them.

✓ Make sure your potential mentor develops a plan that suits your schedule and your time frame of completion. Interview and ask questions. Be specific in your descriptions of proposed outcomes.

✓ Be sure you can develop a relationship with your mentor that allows you both to be real and comfortable. Have fun together. Chemistry is critical as it will enhance your willingness to do the hard things and make them more palatable when the going gets tough.

✓ Commit to a specific period of time. Be disciplined and see that commitment through to its conclusion. Often the results that we desire will require that we make some changes in ourselves. Personal changes don't usually happen overnight and you must be willing to allow the time that it takes to make those changes.

✓ Learn to trust your mentor and be willing to be uncomfortable. You may not always understand and that's okay. Do the uncomfortable until it becomes comfortable.

## Waiting is the Hardest Part

In the achievement of any goal—especially big ones—it can be hard to keep your motivation up while you're waiting for the goal to be accomplished. The key is to focus on staying INSPIRED instead of MOTIVATED.

The definition of the word "inspire" means "to breathe life into." When you are inspired, you breathe life back into your plan.

Motivation is internal. It relates to your personal internal MOTIVE for doing something. Why? What do you have to gain? What emotion is connected to your action?

Inspiration is the bigger vision. Motivation is more practical and tactical. You need both. Here are some examples of Inspiration and Motivation, as they relate to goals.

## Money

Your inspiration is that you want to have the lifestyle that a wealthy person has. You may want their toys, or the quality of life that a person with stable finances has. You're looking outside yourself to be inspired. "I want to live like that."

Your motivation, then, is personal. "I am motivated to set aside 10% of my income for savings, get rid of my debt, stop using credit cards."

## Health

Your inspiration can be someone who is fit and trim, someone who is really old and healthy, someone who's overcome a physical challenge.

Your motivation, then, is "I am motivated to exercise, eat right, get more sleep," et cetera.

## Relationships

**Inspiration:** You want to be like your parents who were married for 50 years, or that old couple in the park holding hands.
**Motivation:** I am motivated to be a better partner, or to actively seek out new relationships.

---

*Inspiration is the vision; motivation is what propels you to take the action. Motivation can wane, but Inspiration can give it back to you.*

---

## The Productivity Accelerator System

As mentioned, we've created a system called The Productivity Accelerator that can help you bust out of bad habits and procrastination, and integrate all of the key areas talked about so far in the chapter into your daily life.

Why do we procrastinate? Most often, people procrastinate things for one of three reasons.

1. They don't want to do it in the first place (like getting your taxes ready).
2. They don't know how to do it (like recaulking the bathtub).
3. They haven't fit it into their schedule.

This system corrects all three. First of all, you'll be able to see what things you are avoiding. If something keeps showing up, and you're not doing it, you'll take a closer look. If it is something you don't want to do, delegate it. If you can't, then you can plan it for a time when you are most likely to do it. If it is something you don't know how to do, plan to learn how! You will never again be faced with not being able to fit something into your schedule.

Sure, there are more complex systems of time management out there. You may be looking at this and wondering, why is this going to work? It's no more complicated than a fancy To-Do List. Yes and no. This system will work perfectly well in conjunction with other high tech and complex systems of productivity. You can use this with any of the apps available on the market. But, when it comes to getting stuff done, there is one important rule to follow:

*The less you have to think about it*
*the more time you have to actually do things!*

Give the system two weeks. Most people find that their productivity is literally doubled in the two weeks. That is, if you are getting 10 things done a week now, in two weeks you might be completing 20!

## How to Use the System

This simple system is comprised of three elements. The Master To-Do list, Moments of Transition, and Your Productivity Partner. Each week, preferably Sunday night or Monday morning, you'll write your items in your Master To-Do List. Once completed, you'll send (scan or e-mail) this list to your Productivity Partner. Throughout the week you'll cross off items as you do them. At the end of the week, meet with your Productivity Partner (by phone or in person) and let them know how you did. That's it! It's a simple, but powerful system.

## Picking Your "To-Do" Items

What kinds of things should you put on your Master To-Do List? Everything! Don't go crazy with the details, but basically put on this list everything you need to do in the week. Need to wash your car? Put it on the list. Want to exercise three times this week? Put it on the list. Do you have a goal to read more? Put it on the list!

Put items on your list that relate to each of your major goals in life. For example, your major goals in life might be to: a) Build my business. b) Get in shape, c) Spend time with my kids, and d) Practice my spiritual growth. So, on my list each week you put things like marketing, exercise, taking the kids to the beach, and writing in your journal.

There is no need to put recurring events like school or work on the list. This list is for things you want to make sure you get done that wouldn't happen otherwise.

Make sure that the items on your list are broken down into small enough parts. For example, don't write "Work on book." That's too big. One of the pleasures of the system is checking off completed actions. Instead, break it down to individual parts: Write Introduction of book, Finish Chapter One, etc. . . .

The elements of a good action step are that it is **observable** and **completable**. In other words, you have to be able to DO it, and you have to be able to FINISH it. Exercise, clean the house, write a report—these are good action items. You can see yourself doing them, and you can tell when they are finished.

Improve self esteem, be a better mother, be healthy—these are neither observable nor measurable.

It's okay to put more on the list than you can get done in a week—as long as you don't beat yourself up about it! The idea here is to stretch yourself a little.

## Your Productivity Partner

An essential component of the Productivity Accelerator is your Productivity Partner. The main reason the system works is because of the accountability provided by your Productivity Partner.

This system was developed within the context of Personal and Executive Coaching. Ideally, you'll have a professional coach who can help you select To-Do items that will speed you toward your goals. Similarly, a coach can help you see trends in things you do or don't do.

For example, when Mick started working with a coach, his coach noticed that he kept saying he was going to exercise, and then he never "found the time". The coach helped Mick to see that it wasn't about the time—there was a limiting belief. Once he saw that, he was able to start exercising. This wouldn't have happened if he'd kept telling himself, "I'll get to it later . . ."

Don't worry. The system works perfectly well even if you don't have a professional coach. You can buddy up with someone else. What are the qualities of a perfect Productivity Partner?

A PERFECT PRODUCTIVITY PARTNER IS:

- Able to meet via phone or in person once a week.
- Supportive of your goals (and non-judgmental).
- Honest enough to challenge you when you are making excuses.
- Gentle enough that you'll want to call them each week.
- Willing to commit to being your partner for at least six months.

## The Most Important Component

Of all the components in the Productivity Accelerator, the most important is that you USE it. We call this *Moments of Transition.* Here's how to use them.

At the moments of transition in your day, when you have just finished one activity and are about to start another, refer to the Master To-Do List. Make sure the activity you are about to engage in is on your list. Here are two scenarios: one where you have more time than you'd planned, and one where you have less.

**SCENARIO ONE:**

Sharon has been using the Productivity Accelerator for two weeks. One morning, she receives an e-mail that the morning meeting she has planned was cancelled. Suddenly, she has an extra two hours in her day. Should she:

a. Put on her bikini and head to the beach?
b. Turn on the news to see what's happening in the world?
c. Go into the kitchen and make a snack?
d. Look at her Master To Do List and see what else she can do?

Of course, the answer is D. Sharon looks at her list and decides that this would be a good chance to do some office filing. Before she knows it, she's knocked four things off her list!

This is the first key to productivity. ALWAYS WORK FROM YOUR MASTER TO-DO LIST.

This is not to say that you can't ever "veg out" on the couch. But, if you look at your list you'll probably find something you can do relatively quickly. You'll be more motivated if you just look at the list!

SCENARIO TWO:

Tony is an artist. He has been using the Productivity Accelerator for a month and is thrilled with the increase in the amount of stuff he's getting done. Today, he is meeting with his web designer on the layout for his new website. There is an accident on the highway on his way back home, and he's running forty-five minutes late. Now he's not going to have time to stop at the market for groceries before he picks his daughter up from school. What should he do?

a. Drive through fast food—*again*!
b. Stress out and start yelling at the traffic.
c. Set his alarm for midnight so he can go to the all night market.
d. Look at his Master To-Do list.

Of course, the answer is D. Looking at the list, Tony will be able to rearrange his plan so that he can go to the market, or make a plan for dinner and go another day. The second key to productivity is to USE A CALENDAR.

Plan out your To-Do List items. Need to take the cat to the vet? When? What day is laundry day this week? Put it on your calendar. Use pencil! The key is flexibility. If something comes up and you are delayed, you can rearrange your calendar to fit everything in.

So, in the previous scenario, Tony picks up his daughter and goes home. He realizes that he has enough food to make a quick dinner, and then after dinner he washes his car (which was on his list for tomorrow). Now he doesn't have to do that tomorrow, and he can go to the market then!

The most critical time in time management is the Moment of Transition.

---

*The difference between successful people and unsuccessful people is how they manage that Moment of Transition.*

---

## Final Exam

Let's see if you're ready to put the Productivity Accelerator to use!

Denise is a student. She hasn't started the Productivity Accelerator yet. She knows she wants to get in shape and make some more money. What does she do to get started?

a. Fill out her weekly Master To-Do List with observable, completable goals.
b. Arrange a Productivity Partner to exchange lists with.
c. Plan her calendar using the list.
d. Refer to her Master To-Do list during the Moments of Transition.
e. All of the above.

Of course, the answer is A. Then, at the end of the week, Denise will send her list to her buddy and they'll go over it. She will be amazed at how much stuff she got done.

Are you ready to start using The Productivity Accelerator? You can make copies of the worksheet that appears on the next page.

# Master To Do List

Check boxes when item is completed

Spiritual:

- ______ ☐
- ______ ☐
- ______ ☐
- ______ ☐
- ______ ☐
- ______ ☐

Work/School:

- ______ ☐
- ______ ☐
- ______ ☐
- ______ ☐
- ______ ☐
- ______ ☐

Family:

- ______ ☐
- ______ ☐
- ______ ☐
- ______ ☐
- ______ ☐
- ______ ☐

Personal:

- ______ ☐
- ______ ☐
- ______ ☐
- ______ ☐
- ______ ☐
- ______ ☐

Friends:

- ______ ☐
- ______ ☐
- ______ ☐
- ______ ☐
- ______ ☐
- ______ ☐

Financial:

- ______ ☐
- ______ ☐
- ______ ☐
- ______ ☐
- ______ ☐
- ______ ☐

At the end of each week, scan/email to your Productivity Partner

Well, there you have it! The GROW! System for Change. In Part Three, you'll take everything you've learned in the book and develop your own action plan for achieving your goals in 30 days.

# Part Three

## *The 30 Day GROW! Challenge*

# Overview of the 30 Day GROW! Challenge

This is it—where the pedal meets the metal. You're about to embark on a transformational journey that will overhaul some of the key areas of your life, using the GROW! System.

You might be thinking, "There's no way I can achieve all of my goals in 30 days." And, you'd be right. For some goals, it will take significantly longer than that. But what you CAN do is get a great head start and lay the foundation for the months to come.

No matter where you are starting, or how far you have to go, you are going to grow in the next 30 days, if you follow the program. Guaranteed. 100% can't fail, guaranteed.

You're probably getting excited to start. You want to pick a day and jump into it. But, if you're one of those people who just flipped to this part of the book so you could get started, we are going to ask you to wait.

Read the first two parts of the book first. Do the exercises. Learn the concepts Don't just flip to this half of the book and jump in. You know what the experts say, "If you want the same results, do the same things. If you want to change your life, you need to change."

The first two parts of this book set a critical foundation for change. If you don't understand why you need to change, and what you need to do to make the changes happen—and stick—any change you make will be short lived.

Having said that, let's do it!

# Pre-Challenge Prep Day

Today is the day you'll get prepared for the next four weeks. After all, you need to figure out what you're going to grow if you're going to plant a garden.

In the following spaces, write down the three goals you identified earlier in the book. Then, come up with some concrete, measurable results that are realistic to attain in thirty days. So, if you are losing weight, don't say you're going to lose fifty pounds in four weeks. But don't only say five pounds, either. Choose a number that is reasonable, and yet a stretch. Eight to ten pounds in four weeks is reasonable.

Similarly, if you have another kind of goal, make sure that you word it in such a way that it's measurable. "Be a better dad" is not measurable. "Spend twenty hours with my kids" is measurable.

Goal #1: ________________________________________

This is what I'd like to accomplish in the next 30 days

________________________________________

________________________________________

________________________________________

Goal #2: ______________________________

This is what I'd like to accomplish in the next 30 days

______________________________

______________________________

______________________________

Goal #3: ______________________________

This is what I'd like to accomplish in the next 30 days

______________________________

______________________________

______________________________

Also, on the last day of the challenge, you'll have a "Post Challenge Reward Day." Choose three decent sized rewards that relate to your goals that you can treat yourself with at the end of the month. Note that you don't want to choose something that will set you back. In other words, if you're losing weight, don't choose a huge cheat meal. Choose to go shopping for some new clothes. Identify goals that will SUPPORT your growth, not reverse it.

Write down the three rewards here:

Goal #1: ______________________________

This is my Post Challenge Reward:

______________________________

______________________________

______________________________

Goal #2: ______________________________________________

This is my Post Challenge Reward:

________________________________________________________

________________________________________________________

________________________________________________________

Goal #3: ______________________________________________

This is my Post Challenge Reward:

________________________________________________________

________________________________________________________

________________________________________________________

# Week One: GROW! Your Mind

## Day One: You Can Do This. The 4 Ss.

As we learned in the book, before we can move forward on our goals, we need to lay the foundation with Pre-Goal Setting.

There are four pillars to Pre Goal Setting.

- PILLAR ONE: SELF-ACCEPTANCE

First you must accept yourself and your desire to grow and improve.

HOW TO: Write down accomplishments from your professional life as motivation to keep achieving. Remember, there is more you can accomplish when you put your mind to it.

________________________________________

________________________________________

________________________________________

________________________________________

________________________________________

- PILLAR TWO: SELF-RESPECT

We often need reminding that we already have the skills and qualities to reach our goals.

HOW TO: Take time to reflect on what you are most proud of about yourself. Write down the positive qualities, characteristics, and traits that you possess.

______________________________________________

______________________________________________

______________________________________________

______________________________________________

______________________________________________

- PILLAR THREE: SELF-CONFIDENCE

During a struggle, it is easy to forget our past accomplishments.

HOW TO: Write down situations when you used your positive qualities. This will help you build confidence and resilience.

______________________________________________

______________________________________________

______________________________________________

______________________________________________

______________________________________________

- PILLAR FOUR: SELF DIRECTION

Think about the areas where you need most improvement, such as time management or taking initiative.

HOW TO: What changes do you need to make? Write them down.

______________________________________________

______________________________________________

______________________________________________

______________________________________________

______________________________________________

## Day Two: Vision

Now that you've done the Pre-Work, it's time to set your vision.

### THE THREE Ps OF A POWERFUL VISION

Here are some tips on how to set a powerful vision.

*Present tense,* as though we have already achieved our vision.

*Powerful language,* using motivating words and concepts.

*Positive outcomes,* avoiding qualifiers like "if, could, might . . ." and relating what will be happening rather than what we won't be doing. For example, "I have stopped . . ." is not a positive outcome

Write your vision in the following space.

________________________________________

________________________________________

________________________________________

________________________________________

________________________________________

## Day Three: Establishing a Personal Growth Philosophy

Yesterday, you created a Personal Vision. Today, we take it one step further by expanding it into a Personal Growth Philosophy that can be carried with you throughout your life, across different goals. This isn't about having a vision for the future, as much as it is crafting a core philosophy that reflects who you are.

As an example, here is Oprah Winfrey's statement: "To be a teacher. And to be known for inspiring my students to be more than they thought they could be."

Here is Richard Branson's: "To have fun in [my] journey through life and learn from [my] mistakes."

To help you get started, complete the following statements.

I am at my best when . . .

________________________________________

________________________________________

I am at my worst when . . .

________________________________________

________________________________________

I am truly happy when . . .

________________________________________

________________________________________

My deepest positive emotions come when . . .

My greatest talents and best gifts are . . .

When all is said and done, the most important things in life are . . .

Creating a Personal Growth Philosophy requires deep reflection about who we are and what our purpose is. In the space provided below create your Personal Growth Philosophy. Draw heavily upon the thinking you've done in the previous steps.

Review your Personal Growth Philosophy and ask yourself the following questions. Does it . . .

- Bring out the best in me?
- Challenge and motivate me?
- Communicate my vision and values?
- Address significant roles in my life?
- Express timelines, proven principles that produce quality of life results?
- Represent the unique contribution I can make to society?

If not, rework it!

## Develop a Tagline

Businesses have taglines. Here are the elements of an effective tagline, using some past and current business taglines.

1. Should be memorable. But it has to resonate with the vision for the brand.
    a. Wheaties *The breakfast of champions.*
    b. United Negro College Fund *The mind is a terrible thing to waste.*
    c. Tyco *A valuable part of your world.*

2. Has to include a key benefit.
    a. Verizon Wireless *Can you hear me now? . . . Good.*

3. Differentiate the brand from the competition while creating positive feelings about the brand. Lea & Perrins: "Steak sauce only a cow could hate"
   a. US Marines *The few, the proud, the Marines.*

4. It should be unique and specific, not bland and boring. "We're the best!"
   a. Taco Bell *Yo quiero Taco Bell.*

5. Define the target market.
   a. Trix Cereal *Silly rabbit, Trix are for kids.*

So let's look at some taglines of some of the key names in the personal growth industry. Then, we'll get into how to develop a personal tagline for some of your most important goals.

Tony Robbins: *Life on your terms.*

Bob Proctor: *Tell me what you want and I'll show you how to get it.*

Marc David: *Visionary nutrition reuniting science and soul.*

Mark Hyman: *Medicine for the future.*

John Cummuta: *Transforming Debt into Wealth.*

Brian Tracy: *Achieve your personal and business goals faster.*

Earl Nightingale: *You become what you think about.*

David Bach: *Live Rich, finish rich.*

Gregg Braden: *bridging the gap between ancient wisdom and technology.*

Sonia Choquette: *I believe the sixth sense should be the first.*

Marshall Goldsmith, *"Life is good."*

Dale Carnegie, *"Real transformation begins within."*

Now it's your turn to develop your own personal tagline.

Remember, it has to make you FEEL GOOD. It has to have power, and passion. And be memorable. Not, "I am so happy and grateful that I have an income of $1 million dollars and am easily living at my goal weight." That's an affirmation not a tagline.

Here are some examples:
"My life, my terms."
"Life. In balance."
"Work hard, play hard."
"I run every day, rain or shine."

"I never miss deadlines. Period."
"Whatever it takes."
"LOVE what makes you healthy."

Now, use your Personal Growth Philosophy to create a compelling one sentence tagline that sums up who you are as a person and what you believe in. Write it here:

______________________________________________

______________________________________________

______________________________________________

______________________________________________

______________________________________________

## Day Four: Mind Alignment

In Chapter Seven we learned about the Johari Window, and identified four "windows" where we can get stuck. Today, for each one of your goals, apply the Johari Window to realign your thinking and behaviors.

### PRIVATE SELF

In this quadrant, identify the behaviors that you know in your heart of hearts you are doing that need to change. These are the things you do when no one else is looking, and keep you from achieving your goal.

Goal One: ________________________________________

________________________________________________

Goal Two: ________________________________________

________________________________________________

Goal Three: ______________________________________

________________________________________________

### PUBLIC SELF

In this quadrant, identify the things you are doing publicly because you are concerned with status, image, what other people think of you, et cetera, that may not be in alignment with your goals.

Goal One: ________________________________________

________________________________________________

Goal Two: ______________________________

______________________________

Goal Three: ______________________________

______________________________

UNKNOWN

For this quadrant, choose a trusted advisor who has already achieved the goal you want to achieve. Ask him or her, "What are some of the things you did to achieve the goal? How did you stop doing the behaviors that weren't in alignment with the goal?" In other words, right now, there are behaviors that you may not know about, and the trusted advisor doesn't know if you do or don't do them. But, asking the questions can reveal otherwise hidden information and ideas. Write them down here:

Goal One: ______________________________

______________________________

Goal Two: ______________________________

______________________________

Goal Three: ______________________________

______________________________

## BLIND SPOT

Ask your trusted advisor, "What are the things that you see me do that are keeping me from achieving my goals, that I may not be aware of?" Write them down here:

Goal One: ______________________________

________________________________________

Goal Two: ______________________________

________________________________________

Goal Three: ____________________________

________________________________________

## Day Five: Taking Control of Your Emotions

Today we are going to manage the emotions that people tend to feel as they are experiencing personal growth. Remember, the stages of Emotional Change are:

1. Depression/Frustration/Anger
2. Resolve/Excitement/Elation
3. The Letdown/Blues
4. Impatience/Frustration
5. Sadness/Fear of the Future

Here is a list of common negative emotions.

| ***Uneasy*** | ***Angry*** | ***Frightened*** |
|---|---|---|
| nervous | frustrated | uneasy |
| tense | cross | weak |
| anxious | irritated | insecure |
| flustered | annoyed | inadequate |
| insecure | furious | tense |
| angry | livid | anxious |
| cross | enraged | nervous |
| confused | hurt | scared |
| bored | inadequate | petrified |
| flat | trapped | threatened |
| apathetic | tired | trapped |
| weak | scared | horrified |

***Happy***
pleased
glad
wonderful
elated
excited
content
surprised
proud
relieved
satisfied
confident

***Unhappy***
hurt
upset
lonely
guilty
miserable
bereft
despairing
devastated
lost
down

***Confused***
hurt
upset
lonely
inadequate
cross
miserable
shocked
mixed-up
nervous
scared
discontented
foolish

***Negative***
distrustful
suspicious
scornful
disdain
bitter
stupid
shame
worthless

***Upset***
angry
frustrated
sad
tearful
hurt
miserable
weepy

For each of your three goals, write down a sentence that describes how you feel (or might feel) in each of these Stages of Emotional Change.

Goal One:

1. Depression/Frustration/Anger

______________________________

2. Resolve/Excitement/Elation

______________________________

3. The Letdown/Blues

______________________________

4. Impatience/Frustration

______________________________

5. Sadness/Fear of the Future

______________________________

Goal Two:

1. Depression/Frustration/Anger

______________________________

2. Resolve/Excitement/Elation

______________________________

3. The Letdown/Blues

______________________________

4. Impatience/Frustration

______________________________

5. Sadness/Fear of the Future

______________________________

Goal Three:

1. Depression/Frustration/Anger

______________________________

2. Resolve/Excitement/Elation

______________________________

3. The Letdown/Blues

______________________________

4. Impatience/Frustration

______________________________

5. Sadness/Fear of the Future

______________________________

Tomorrow we'll use this list to transform the things you say to yourself about these emotions.

## Day Six: Transforming Self-Talk

Yesterday, you identified some emotions that relate to your personal growth and the achievement of your goals. Today we are going to take those emotions and use them to identify the thoughts and inner self-talk you have that can sabotage your progress.

Remember, we said that negative thought patterns occur because of:

1. Attachment to things.
2. Expectations of others.
3. Expectations of yourself.
4. Attachment to a different time.
5. The idea that things should be different than they are.

For each of your goals, identify a current negative self-talk statement that you tell yourself. This can either be about your current state ("I am terrible at my job . . .") or one about the future ("I'll never be able to get a better job.")

Goal One: ________________________________________

__________________________________________________

Goal Two: ________________________________________

__________________________________________________

Goal Three: ______________________________________

__________________________________________________

Next, in the following spaces, identify which of the negative thought patterns the self-talk relates to. For example, "I am terrible at my job" comes from "expectations of yourself." "I'll never be able to get another job" can be attachment to a different time or expectations of others.

Goal One: ______________________________________

______________________________________

Goal Two: ______________________________________

______________________________________

Goal Three: ______________________________________

______________________________________

Finally, use the Self Correction Script to change your self talk.

SELF-CORRECTION SCRIPT:

"This isn't like me. Normally, I am ____________."

"This isn't like me. Normally I am good at my job. I am still in my learning curve."

"This isn't like me. Normally I don't worry about the future."

Goal One: ______________________________________

______________________________________

Goal Two: ______________________________________________

______________________________________________

Goal Three: ______________________________________________

______________________________________________

## Day Seven: Week One Reflection

Goal #1: ______________________________

Here's What I Accomplished This Week

______________________________

______________________________

______________________________

______________________________

______________________________

Goal #2: ______________________________

Here's What I Accomplished This Week

______________________________

______________________________

______________________________

______________________________

______________________________

Goal #3: ______________________________

Here's What I Accomplished This Week

______________________________

______________________________

______________________________

______________________________

______________________________

# Week Two: GROW! Your Health

This week is all about your health! By the end of the week, you'll have a personalized system (and a head start!) on making your body as healthy as it can be.

## Day One: What Needs to Go Versus What Needs to Grow

Today, you'll identify some health behaviors you need to give up, and some that you want to implement (or do more often).

Here are some examples of things to give up:

- Watching TV every night.
- Reading your phone in the middle of the night.
- Drinking soda every day.
- Drinking alcohol every day.
- Staying up too late.
- Eating fast food every week.

Here are some examples of things you might want to grow:

- Getting 7–8 hours of sleep a night.
- Eating fresh fruit every day.
- Eating more vegetables.
- Drinking 8 glasses of water a day.
- Exercising 20 minutes a day.

Now it's your turn. In the following spaces, write down some behaviors that need to go, and some that need to grow.

NEED TO GO

______________________________________________

______________________________________________

______________________________________________

______________________________________________

______________________________________________

______________________________________________

NEED TO GROW

______________________________________________

______________________________________________

______________________________________________

______________________________________________

______________________________________________

______________________________________________

## Day Two: The Water Challenge

According to the American Council on Fitness, "Water not only composes 75 percent of all muscle tissue and about 10 percent of fatty tissue, it also acts within each cell to transport nutrients and dispel waste. And, because water composes more than half of the human body, it is impossible to sustain life for more than a week without it." Not surprisingly, humans can go for more than a week without soda.

Your body will get adjusted to a constant state of dehydration. This means you might be dehydrated and not even know it! By the time you're thirsty, you're already dehydrated! So, drink up that water!

Also, while water is very important for your health, there are some times when drinking too much water can be a problem: If you have any kidney or adrenal problems, or your doctor has you taking diuretics, you need to consult with your doctor about how much water to drink each day.

Here are some tips for the Water Challenge:

Do you have enough water? Get a container that you can fill with water and take with you. Make sure that you have a source of clean, fresh water.

One mistake you might make is to forget to bring water with you. It's a pain to have to buy water when you know you have some at home! Put a sticky note to remind you to bring water, or place your car keys near your container of water.

Go slowly. Increase your hydration by only four ounces at first. That's it. Drink just four ounces more than you usually do!

Many of the "enhanced" water drinks on the market are full of crap. If you choose to consume "vitamin water," make sure that there is no high-fructose corn syrup or a lot of added sugar. Honestly, fresh, plain water is still the best choice.

Did you know that hydration can help the muscle soreness that accompanies exercise? Drinking water can flush out the lactic acid build-up that happens when you exercise your muscles. You'll be less sore and for a shorter period of time!

Don't drink all of the water you need per day all at once. Divide the amount you need and drink several glasses of water throughout the day. This is especially important if you engage in lots of heavy exercise.

If you're finding yourself making excuses like "I don't like water" maybe you tried to add in too much too soon. If you're having trouble drinking all your water, scale back your goal.

Don't substitute other drinks for water, though. The key is to develop a taste for the $H_2O$. Don't forget, you probably didn't like coffee or alcohol the first time you tried them either! It took time for you to like them. This time, learn to love something healthy!

You can learn to love drinking water. Really. Just keep drinking it, and pretty soon nothing will taste as good as a refreshing glass of $H_2O$.

Drink a glass at every transition point in the day—when you wake up, when you leave for work, when you get to work, et cetera.

Drink a glass of water before every meal.

When at a party, have one glass of water for every alcoholic beverage.

Drink sparkling water in a nice glass during dinner.

Carry water with you everywhere.

## Day Three: What Healthy Foods Do You Love?

All too often we get into a food rut; eating the same old things every day. Today, you'll identify which healthy foods you like, and then commit to adding some of them into your diet. Circle the foods you like, cross out the ones you are allergic to or go against dietary restrictions, and put a star next to the ones you haven't tried.

VEGETABLES

Asparagus
Avocados
Beet greens
Beets
Bell peppers
Bok Choy
Broccoli
Brussels sprouts
Cabbage
Carrots
Cauliflower
Celery
Collard Greens
Corn, Fresh Sweet
Cucumbers
Eggplant
Fennel
Garlic
Green beans
Green peas
Kale
Leeks
Mushrooms, crimini
Mushrooms, shiitake
Mustard greens
Olive oil, extra virgin
Olives
Onions
Potatoes
Romaine lettuce
Sea vegetables
Spinach
Squash, summer
Squash, winter
Sweet potatoes
Swiss chard
Tomatoes
Turnip greens

### NUTS & SEEDS

Almonds
Cashews
Flaxseeds
Peanuts
Pumpkin seeds
Sesame seeds
Sunflower seeds
Walnuts

### FRUITS

Apples
Apricots
Bananas
Blueberries
Cantaloupe
Cranberries
Figs
Grapefruit
Grapes
Kiwifruit
Lemon/Limes
Oranges
Papaya
Pears
Pineapple
Plums & Prunes
Raspberries
Strawberries
Watermelon

### BEANS & LEGUMES

Black beans
Dried peas
Garbanzo beans (chickpeas)
Kidney beans
Lentils
Lima beans
Miso
Navy beans
Pinto beans
Soy sauce
Soybeans
Tempeh
Tofu

### POULTRY & MEATS

Beef, grass-fed
Chicken, pasture-raised
Lamb, grass-fed
Turkey, pasture-raised
Eggs & Dairy
Cheese, grass-fed
Cow's milk, grass-fed
Eggs, pasture-raised
Yogurt, grass-fed

### SEAFOOD

Cod
Salmon
Sardines
Scallops
Shrimp
Tuna

### GRAINS

Barley
Brown rice
Buckwheat
Millet
Oats
Quinoa
Rye
Whole wheat

Then, write down five foods you will commit to eating in the next week.

1. ______________________________
2. ______________________________
3. ______________________________
4. ______________________________
5. ______________________________

## Day Four: Exercise = Motion & Emotion

Today is all about getting your move on. There is plenty of research that shows that exercise reduces stress, releases "feel good" hormones, and boost overall vitality. We're not suggesting that you sign up for an Iron Man competition (unless you want to). But, integrating some motion into your everyday life can do wonders for the mind and body.

### HERE ARE SOME TIPS TO ADD MORE MOTION INTO YOUR LIFE.

- Go to the playground with your kids. If you don't have kids, borrow some! When was the last time you were on the swings?
- Turn on the music and have a dance party. Some old Motown can work wonders for the body, mind, and soul.
- Every weekend, choose one project that will give your body some "non-exercise" exercise. Gardening, mowing the lawn, cleaning out the garage, scrubbing the floors—these are all great forms of exercise that are productive too.
- You don't need a gym membership to exercise. Do some old-fashioned calisthenics—jumping jacks, pushups, sit-ups, stretches. It uses your own body weight to get you fit!
- Take a fun class. If you're in the park doing some yoga moves with a bunch of other people, you might just forget you're exercising!

- At work, take a walk during breaks, get outside (if the weather is nice enough) and get some fresh air. You'll return in a better mood, with a clearer head.

What are some ways you can integrate more moving around in your life?

I can commit to __________ minutes of exercise a day. If I have trouble focusing at work, I will try exercising before work for __________ minutes (recommended minimum of twenty minutes) to see if it helps me concentrate better.

## Day Five: Stress Management

Stress can be a major inhibitor of personal growth. Today we'll look at what stresses you out, how it affects your health, and what you can do about it.

### What Do You Get Stressed About?

School or Work stress

________________________________________

________________________________________

________________________________________

Social stress

________________________________________

________________________________________

________________________________________

Family stress

________________________________________

________________________________________

________________________________________

Which of the following major effects of stress do you experience? (Check all that apply.)

**Physical**

- ☐ headaches
- ☐ stomach aches
- ☐ dizziness
- ☐ back pain
- ☐ neck stiffness
- ☐ ulcer sores on mouth

- ☐ jaw pains
- ☐ weight loss
- ☐ weight gain
- ☐ twitches (eyelids, face)
- ☐ weakness
- ☐ nausea
- ☐ indigestion
- ☐ excessive sleeping
- ☐ aggressiveness
- ☐ rapid or difficult breathing
- ☐ skin problems
- ☐ constant fatigue
- ☐ cold hands or feet
- ☐ excessive sweating
- ☐ chest pains
- ☐ high blood pressure

**Emotional**

- ☐ mood changes
- ☐ lack of concentration
- ☐ nightmares
- ☐ panic attacks
- ☐ anxiety
- ☐ anger
- ☐ irritability
- ☐ crying
- ☐ thoughts of suicide
- ☐ depression
- ☐ confusion
- ☐ feelings of helplessness
- ☐ restlessness
- ☐ racing thoughts
- ☐ loss of appetite

**Behavioral**

- ☐ smoking
- ☐ nail biting
- ☐ tapping
- ☐ pulling hair
- ☐ grinding teeth
- ☐ use of alcohol
- ☐ use of medication
- ☐ compulsive dieting
- ☐ hair chewing
- ☐ nervous laughter
- ☐ pacing
- ☐ lateness
- ☐ putting things off
- ☐ overeating
- ☐ compulsive overeating

## Relaxation Techniques

One powerful way to reduce stress is to use relaxation techniques. One of these is to create a relaxing place that you can mentally go to anytime you're feeling stressed out.

### YOUR RELAXING PLACE

What does it look like?

_______________________________________________

_______________________________________________

_______________________________________________

Do you associate any sounds with your relaxing place?

_______________________________________________

_______________________________________________

_______________________________________________

What does your relaxing place feel like?

_______________________________________________

_______________________________________________

_______________________________________________

What does your relaxing place smell like?

_______________________________________________

_______________________________________________

_______________________________________________

What are its emotional components? (Safety, calmness ...)

________________________________________

________________________________________

________________________________________

### TEACH YOUR BODY TO RELAX

- Exercise that controls the body and releases tension like Tai Chi or boxing.
- Deep breathing.
- Yoga.
- Meditation.
- Warm, long baths or showers.
- My relaxing place.

## Day Six: Get Some Sleep!

How did you sleep last night? Research shows that sleep and mood are profoundly connected. In an article in Arch Gen Psychiatry, researchers found that mood may vary with the duration of "prior wakefulness" and time of day.* In other words, how long you've been awake and what time of day it is can determine your mood.

Here are some suggestions for getting good sleep and improving your level of happiness. These tips come from Gretchen Rubin, author of The Happiness Project.**

1. **Set a specific bedtime for yourself.** Many people have no idea what time they "should" go to sleep in order to feel well-rested. Be realistic! If you have to wake up at 7:00 am, staying awake until 1:30 am each night is unlikely to be sufficient.

2. **Get ready for bed well before your bedtime.** Sometimes, paradoxically, I feel too tired to go to bed. I try to wash my face and brush my teeth well before I plan to turn off the light.

3. **Make your room very dark.** Shut the blinds, block out the lights from your computer, clock, phone, etc. Even the tiny light from a digital alarm clock can disrupt a sleep cycle.

---

* https://www.ncbi.nlm.nih.gov/m/pubmed/9040282/

** https://www.gretchenrubin.com/

4. **Stretch.** A study showed that women who were having trouble sleeping fared much better when they stretched four times a week.

5. **Keep your bedroom a little chilly.**

6. If your mind is racing with worry, **make a list of everything you need to do the next day**. This really works for me. I can make myself crazy fretting that I'm going to forget to do something important; if I make a list, I can relax.

7. **Tidy up your bedroom.** It's not restful to be surrounded by clutter.

8. **Exercise.** Studies suggest that people who exercise fall asleep faster and stay asleep longer—and this is particularly true for people who have trouble sleeping.

9. **An hour before bedtime, avoid work that requires alert thinking.** I try to stop myself from checking my emails before I go to bed, because it wakes me up. I made this mistake just last night, in fact. I got some emails answered, but I was so wound up that it took me forever to go to sleep.

10. My personal sleep-inducing innovation: **Slather myself with body lotion.** This feels good and also, if I'm having trouble sleeping because I'm hot, it cools me down.

11. My other sleep-inducing innovation: **Put on socks if my feet are cold.** I feel frumpy, but my husband won't let me use his legs as a foot-warmer.

12. **Yawn.**

13. **Tell yourself, "I have to get up now."** Imagine that you just hit the snooze alarm and in a minute, you're going to be marching through the morning routine. Often this is an exhausting enough prospect to make me fall asleep.

14. **Give up, and re-frame your sleeplessness** as a welcome opportunity to snatch some extra time out of your day. If I wake up and can't get to sleep after 4:00 a.m., I get up and start working. Instead of starting the day feeling annoyed, I have a wonderful feeling of having accomplished a lot before my usual wake-up time of 6:00 a.m.

In the following space, write down some ideas on how you can get better zzzzzs.

______________________________

______________________________

______________________________

______________________________

______________________________

______________________________

## Day Seven: Week Two Reflection

Goal #1: ______________________________

Here's What I Accomplished This Week

______________________________

______________________________

______________________________

______________________________

______________________________

Goal #2: ______________________________

Here's What I Accomplished This Week

______________________________

______________________________

______________________________

______________________________

______________________________

Goal #3: ______________________________

Here's What I Accomplished This Week

______________________________

______________________________

______________________________

______________________________

______________________________

# Week Three:
# GROW! Your Habits

## Day One: Fifteen Day Checkpoint: What is working? What is not?

We are halfway through the 30 days! It's time for a mid-point assessment. How is the plan working for you? What's not working? How can you change it?

What is working:

___

___

___

What is not working:

___

___

___

What needs changing:

___

___

___

## Day Two: Create Your Daily Habits List

Earlier in the month, you made a list of health related behaviors that "need to go" or "need to grow." Expanding on that concept, today you'll make a list of some habits that relate to your goals that you want to put into your life on a daily, weekly, monthly, quarterly, and annual basis.

Here are some examples you might choose from:

Daily

Exercise
Meditate
Journal

Weekly

Go to the Farmer's Market
Declutter one area of your home or office
Call a family member
Write a thank you note

Monthly

Attend a networking meeting
File old papers

Quarterly

Get the car serviced
Update your wardrobe
Get a massage

Annual

Take a vacation with your life partner (or a "staycation")

Get a physical

Perform an annual review of your budget

Strategic Planning Session for next year

Now it's your turn!

Daily

____________________

____________________

____________________

Weekly

____________________

____________________

____________________

Monthly

____________________

____________________

____________________

Quarterly

____________________

____________________

____________________

Annual

---

---

---

## Day Three: Financial Fitness

Today we are going to look at your financial fitness habits. Whether you're a millionaire, or a "dollar'onaire," you can always streamline your financial habits. Here are some examples of financial habits that can help you grow your bank account!

- **Live below your means.** This is so important! If you make $5,000 a month, make sure that your expenses stay below $4,500, for example. Sit down and do the math before you add any permanent expense to your budget.

- **Pay your bills ahead of time.** This is a good financial habit that can save interest fees and prevent late penalties.

- **Read financial books and articles.** Become knowledgeable about money, finance, and investing.

- **Track your spending.** It's very easy to stop off at the drugstore on your way home because you need a bag of cat food, and walk out with $50 in things you forgot you needed. By consistently tracking these items, you'll know exactly where your money is going and be better able to resist impulse buys.

- **Minimize the use of credit.** It's too easy to rack up credit card debt. Instead, save it only for emergencies, and use a debit card or cash for most items.

Now it's your turn. What are some financial habits you can let go of or grow?

________________________________________

________________________________________

________________________________________

________________________________________

________________________________________

________________________________________

## Day Four: Moments of Transition

As we learned earlier in the book, the most powerful times in our day are the moments of transition. It's these times, when you are moving from one activity to another, than can make or break your goals.

Let's look at an example. It's Saturday morning and you just finished your weekly cleaning. You put away the cleaning supplies and look around at the clean house. It's done. This is a moment of transition, and what you do next is vitally important. Do you go sit down on the couch and turn on the TV? Do you call a friend? Do you start a load of laundry?

It's important to note that none of these are necessarily bad. It's perfectly fine to sit down and watch TV. What matters, though, is that you do it with intent. Don't just float from one thing to another. Everyone reading this has probably been sucked down the rabbit hole of watching videos online. You go to look something up and the next thing you know you've been watching News Bloopers for 20 minutes.

Instead, learn to manage those moments of transition by looking at your Productivity Accelerator. Is there anything important you can be doing? Maybe calling your friend is on the list.

In the following spaces, write down some key moments of transition in your day.

Morning:

______________________________________________

______________________________________________

______________________________________________

______________________________________________

Afternoon:

______________________________________________

______________________________________________

______________________________________________

______________________________________________

Evening:

______________________________________________

______________________________________________

______________________________________________

______________________________________________

Weekend:

______________________________________________

______________________________________________

______________________________________________

______________________________________________

## Day Five: Busting Procrastination and Boredom

Yesterday, we identified the key moments of transition. But, sometimes, even if we know WHAT do to, we still don't do it.

Why do we procrastinate? Most often, people procrastinate things for one of three reasons.

1. They don't want to do it in the first place (like getting your taxes ready).
2. They don't know how to do it (like recaulking the bathtub).
3. They haven't fit it into their schedule.

In the following space, write down some things you tend to procrastinate, and the reason you keep putting it off.

______________________________________________

______________________________________________

______________________________________________

______________________________________________

______________________________________________

______________________________________________

Now, for each item, either delegate it, learn how to do it, or put it on your calendar!!

## Day Six: The Productivity Accelerator

Today is the day when you'll finally start using The Productivity Accelerator (if you haven't already been using it). Here's what to do:

1. Fill out your weekly Master To-Do List with observable, completable goals (and the habits to achieve them).
2. Arrange a Productivity Partner to exchange lists with.
3. Plan your calendar using the list.
4. Refer to your Master To-Do list during the Moments of Transition.
5. Send the list to your Productivity Partner at the end of the week.

Remember, a perfect Productivity Partner is

- Able to meet via phone or in person once a week.
- Supportive of your goals (and non-judgmental).
- Honest enough to challenge you when you are making excuses.
- Gentle enough that you'll want to call them each week.
- Willing to commit to being your partner for at least six months.

Who can you ask to be your Productivity Partner? Write some names down in the following space.

________________________________________

________________________________________

________________________________________

________________________________________

# Master To Do List

Check boxes when item is completed

**Spiritual:**

- [ ] ______________________
- [ ] ______________________
- [ ] ______________________
- [ ] ______________________
- [ ] ______________________
- [ ] ______________________

**Work/School:**

- [ ] ______________________
- [ ] ______________________
- [ ] ______________________
- [ ] ______________________
- [ ] ______________________
- [ ] ______________________

**Family:**

- [ ] ______________________
- [ ] ______________________
- [ ] ______________________
- [ ] ______________________
- [ ] ______________________
- [ ] ______________________

**Personal:**

- [ ] ______________________
- [ ] ______________________
- [ ] ______________________
- [ ] ______________________
- [ ] ______________________
- [ ] ______________________

**Friends:**

- [ ] ______________________
- [ ] ______________________
- [ ] ______________________
- [ ] ______________________
- [ ] ______________________
- [ ] ______________________

**Financial:**

- [ ] ______________________
- [ ] ______________________
- [ ] ______________________
- [ ] ______________________
- [ ] ______________________
- [ ] ______________________

At the end of each week, scan/email to your Productivity Partner

## Day Seven: Week Three Reflection

Goal #1: ______________________________

Here's What I Accomplished This Week

______________________________

______________________________

______________________________

______________________________

______________________________

Goal #2: ______________________________

Here's What I Accomplished This Week

______________________________

______________________________

______________________________

______________________________

______________________________

Goal #3: ______________________________

Here's What I Accomplished This Week

______________________________

______________________________

______________________________

______________________________

______________________________

# Week Four: GROW! Your Momentum

## Day One: Concentration

Success Coach Jim Fannin has worked with professional and Olympic athletes in every sport. He identifies the characteristics that gave these high performers the momentum they needed to stay the course. Concentration is a key factor in growing momentum. In his book, The S.C.O.R.E.® Success System, he writes:

"Champions focus their mental and physical energy on each task as it leads to their goals and ultimately their vision. They can especially focus on the basics when the money is on the table. Their competitors can feel this laser-like channeling of energy. This is the killer instinct to narrow one's focus when the game's 'moment of truth' arrives. They can detach from their goals and totally lock in on the task at hand.

"Champions sacrifice other non-golf thoughts so that they can focus all of their energy on their sport and its demands. This has and can result in an imbalance in one's life. Here many champions have faltered.

"*Champions do NOT*: lose focus, get easily distracted, go into the past (except once for swift learning), go into the future (except for strategy and tactics), juggle too many things at once, think outside the arena while performing, get confused or think about their opponent except tactically how to beat them."

Here's what Jim says to do if you find your concentration wavering:

"Re-boot your brain: When thinking negative thoughts or you're replaying the past or projecting too far into the future, do the following: Close your eyes. Unhinge your jaw. Turn your brain off for 10 to 30 seconds. Then open your eyes and send your mind to the next target."

Other tips include the following:

- Bribe your mind: Tell yourself, "I will think about that in 20 minutes when I am done with this."
- Take a nap: Similar to re-booting your brain, if you lie down for 15 minutes, you can usually wake up more focused.
- Keep your eye on the horizon. Remind yourself of the end result of your activity. Why are you doing this? Sometimes stepping back and remembering your vision is enough to get your focus back.

Stay focused today!

## Day Two: Get in the Zone

In an earlier section of the book we talked about the difference between the Comfort Zone and The Zone. To get in The Zone, you have to:

1. Have clear goals for what you want to accomplish.
2. Practice!! Make the behaviors automatic.
3. Create an environment where you can concentrate completely and have the appropriate amount of arousal for the task, and your personality.
4. Breathe, relax, and LET GO. Getting in the zone is more about "letting go" that anything.

For each of your three goals, write down what your Comfort Zone is for that area of your life, and what it looks like when you're in The Zone.

Goal One: ______________________________

______________________________

Comfort Zone: ______________________________

______________________________

The Zone: ______________________________

______________________________

Goal Two: ______________________________

______________________________

Comfort Zone: ______________________________

______________________________

The Zone: ______________________________

______________________________

Goal Three: ______________________________________________

______________________________________________

Comfort Zone: ______________________________________________

______________________________________________

The Zone: ______________________________________________

______________________________________________

## Day Three: Recruit Your Team

Throughout this book we have encouraged you to reach out to others who can help you succeed in your personal and professional growth. In this section, you can list the names of people who you can be part of your success team. For each one of your goals, list the names of the people who are in the following categories. Note that you can have someone in more than one category, and a person can fill roles for more than one goal.

### Goal One:

People Who Are Role Models

________________________________________

________________________________________

People Who Are Mentors

________________________________________

________________________________________

People Who Are Your Productivity Partners

________________________________________

________________________________________

People Who Care

________________________________________

________________________________________

People Who Confront

People with Expertise

People with Social Contacts

People to Play with

People Who Feed Your Need for Community

**Goal Two:**

People Who Are Role Models

People Who Are Mentors

People Who Are Your Productivity Partners

________________________________________________

________________________________________________

People Who Care

________________________________________________

________________________________________________

People Who Confront

________________________________________________

________________________________________________

People with Expertise

________________________________________________

________________________________________________

People with Social Contacts

________________________________________________

________________________________________________

People to Play with

________________________________________________

________________________________________________

People Who Feed Your Need for Community

________________________________________________

________________________________________________

## Goal Three:

People Who Are Role Models

People Who Are Mentors

People Who Are Your Productivity Partners

People Who Care

People Who Confront

People with Expertise

People with Social Contacts

People to Play with

______________________________________________

______________________________________________

People Who Feed Your Need for Community

______________________________________________

______________________________________________

## Day Four: Eliminate Your Energy Drains

Yesterday, we identified the people who can be supportive of your personal and professional growth. Today, let's look at the other side. People, activities, and things that drain your energy and momentum.

**People:** Who are the people in your personal and professional life who drain your energy? Examples might be your boss, your in-laws, irritating coworkers, family members. Write them here.

________________________________________

________________________________________

________________________________________

**Places:** Where are the places you go that drain your energy? Examples might be clubs you belong to, volunteer places that don't feel good anymore, work that is unsatisfying, a cluttered and messy home. Write yours here:

________________________________________

________________________________________

________________________________________

**Things:** Are there things in your life that drain your energy with their upkeep? Examples might be your car, electronics, a garden. Write yours here:

________________________________________

________________________________________

________________________________________

## Day Five: Celebrating Victories

As we learned in the earlier parts of the book, positive reinforcement is a powerful motivator. Today, you'll identify some ways you can celebrate, not achieving the whole goal, but for engaging in the behaviors you want to grow. Here are some examples of ways you can celebrate successfully:

- Go to a concert
- Download some new music
- Go to the movies (in the middle of the day!)
- Watch funny videos
- Go to a park and read
- Get a massage
- Have a "paint night" at home with friends
- Take a day off work
- Get a nice haircut
- Hire a housekeeper
- Get yourself a gift card
- Go to the beach

Now it's your turn! What are some ways you can celebrate your success? (Remember, these reinforcers shouldn't derail your success!)

________________________________________

________________________________________

________________________________________

________________________________________

________________________________________

## Day Six: 30 Day Wrap Up

Goal #1: ________________________________________

Here's What I Accomplished in 30 Days

________________________________________

________________________________________

________________________________________

________________________________________

________________________________________

Goal #2: ________________________________________

Here's What I Accomplished in 30 Days

________________________________________

________________________________________

________________________________________

________________________________________

________________________________________

Goal #3: ________________________________________

Here's What I Accomplished in 30 Days

________________________________________

________________________________________

________________________________________

________________________________________

________________________________________

## Day Seven: What's Next?

Goal #1: ______________________________

This is what I'd like to accomplish in the next 30 days

______________________________

______________________________

______________________________

______________________________

______________________________

Goal #2: ______________________________

This is what I'd like to accomplish in the next 30 days

______________________________

______________________________

______________________________

______________________________

______________________________

Goal #3: ______________________________

This is what I'd like to accomplish in the next 30 days

______________________________

______________________________

______________________________

______________________________

______________________________

Add in a new goal?

______________________________

______________________________

______________________________

## Post-Challenge Reward Day

Remember on the first day, you identified three rewards you were going to give yourself post-challenge? It's time! Don't think you have to complete the whole goal in order to reward yourself. These rewards are for making progress. Enjoy!!!

Goal #1: ______________________________

This is my Post Challenge Reward ______________

______________________________________

______________________________________

______________________________________

Goal #2: ______________________________

This is my Post Challenge Reward ______________

______________________________________

______________________________________

______________________________________

Goal #3: ______________________________

This is my Post Challenge Reward ______________

______________________________________

______________________________________

______________________________________

# CONCLUSION

*"If you are not in the process of becoming the person you want to be, you are automatically engaged in becoming the person you don't want to be."*

—Dale Carnegie

Congratulations! You've finished the book. As we mentioned in the beginning, this book isn't only about changing the things that need changing in your life. It's also about being happy every day, while you're growing. And, sometimes the growth comes in changing the way you see your current situation, and recognizing that the seeds of your future life are in your life today.

To that end, you looked at some key components of personal and professional growth. In Part One you discovered that having an *internal locus of control* is key to believing that you can change your life. You learned how *filters* affect your perception, and how changing the filter can help you focus your attention on the areas of life you want to grow.

You learned about Lewin's Equation and that behavior is a function of the person and their environment. You discovered that a growth mindset is necessary in order to achieve goals. And, you learned about the seven traits of change readiness.

After taking the Change Readiness Assessment, you were able to identify whether or not the timing is right for you to grow, and what you can do to strengthen the areas that aren't ready yet.

You also learned the difference between a Comfort Zone and The Zone, and the difference between reasons and excuses.

There are always cycles in life, and patterns of growth are no exception. You became aware of the four key stages of growth, and learned how to navigate through each of them.

You identified Driving Forces and Resisting Forces and then used Lewin's Change Model to strengthen the driving forces through Unfreezing, Moving, and Refreezing.

People do what they are rewarded for doing, and you learned how to use operant conditioning to reinforce and shape the behaviors you want, and don't.

Heider's Balance Theory taught us how to change our attitudes about things by achieving psychological balance.

In Part Two you learned the components of the GROW! System for personal and professional growth. Of course, GROW is an acronym that stands for Goals, Realign, Overcome obstacles, and Work.

But before you launched into GROWing, you had some Pre-Goal Setting work to do. You used the Four Ss of Self Acceptance, Self Respect, Self Confidence, and Self Direction to till the soil of your mental garden.

You learned the Three Ps of a powerful vision, and then created one! You also refreshed your memory on SMART Goals, and discovered the value of writing them down.

After completing the Rate Your Life Questionnaire, you were able to identify a few areas that you wanted to commit to improving. That was the G in GROW.

Next came the R, and you worked on realigning your behaviors with those that will lead to your goals. You took a good, hard look at what is holding you back.

You then used the Johari Window to identify the behaviors that are leading you to or away from personal and professional growth.

After identifying your Private, Public, Unknown, and Blind Spots, you then came up with some tools that will help you succeed.

Growth is never linear, and you learned about the obstacles that you'll face as you grow. From the Five Negative Emotions of Change to Self Defeating Thought Patterns, you learned how to overcome mental and emotional obstacles.

The stories of The Farmer and the Horse, and The Three Umpires taught you that in order to overcome obstacles in our external environment, we need to be like the farmer, and the third umpire. We need to understand that nothing is good or bad until we CALL it good or bad, and instead have the patience to persevere along our chosen course of action.

In the W section of the GROW! System, you learned how to put everything together into a system that you can use every day. From time management to physical health, getting a support system and a success team, you learned how to apply the ideas to your life.

Finally, at the end of Part Two, you learned the difference between inspiration and motivation, and how The Productivity Accelerator can help you stay motivated and on track.

The last part of the book is where you actually started to grow. The seeds were planted, you watered those seeds, and in thirty days were sure to see measurable results. You grew your mind, your health, your habits, and your momentum.

Let's end the book with an old story that illustrates the theme of this book. You can use the power of your mind to change your life, by focusing on the seeds of your future life as they are present in your current life.

## Two Saplings

An eight-year-old boy went to his grandfather and proudly announced, *"I am going to be very successful when I grow up. Can you give me any tips on how to get there?"*

The grandfather nodded, and without saying a word, took the boy by the hand and walked him to a nearby plant nursery.

There, the two of them chose and purchased two small saplings. They returned home and planted one of them in the back yard. The other sapling was placed in a pot and kept indoors.

*"Which one do you think will be the most successful in the future?"* asked the grandfather.

The boy thought for a moment and said, *"The indoor tree. It's protected and safe while the outdoor one has to cope with the elements."*

The grandfather shrugged his shoulders and said, *"We'll see."*

The grandfather carefully tended to both plants and in a few years, the boy, now a teenager came to visit again. *"You never really answered my question from when I was a young boy. How can I become successful when I grow up?"* he asked.

The old man showed the teenager the indoor tree and then took him outside to have a look at the towering tree outside.

*"Which one is greater?"* the grandfather asked.

*"The outside one. But that doesn't make sense, it has to cope with many more challenges than the inside one."*

The grandfather smiled, *"Yes, but the risk of dealing with challenges is worth it as it has the freedom to spread its roots wider and its leaves towards the heavens. Boy, remember this and you will be successful in whatever you do; If you choose the safe option all of your life you will never grow and be all that you can be, but if you are willing to face the world head-on with all of its dangers and challenges, the sky's the limit."*

If you choose the safe, well-worn path, then a life of mediocrity awaits. But if you have the courage to GROW, you will reach your full potential.

www.ingramcontent.com/pod-product-compliance
Lightning Source LLC
LaVergne TN
LVHW010058170826
845678LV00012B/2171

*9781722507640*